M&M's or Skittles
Choosing Today Whom We Will Serve

Paul Schwanke

Copyright © 2019 by Evangelist Paul Schwanke.
All Scripture quotations are from the King James Bible.

First published by Paul Schwanke,
an Independent Baptist evangelist from Phoenix, Arizona.
Evangelist Schwanke is committed to preaching the Bible
and providing materials to assist pastors and local churches
around the world.

All rights reserved. No part of this book may be reproduced,
stored in a retrieval system, or transmitted in any form
or by any means - electronic, mechanical, photocopy, recording,
or otherwise - without the written permission of the author,
except for brief quotations in printed reviews.

Evangelist Paul Schwanke
www.preachthebible.com

Special thanks to Miss Kelly Schwanke
Special thanks to Cathy

ISBN: 9781794683693

Printed in the United States of America

CONTENTS

Preface	v
Introduction	1
Chapter One - A Famine in the Land	5
Chapter Two - Crossroads	13
Chapter Three - Going Home	21
Chapter Four - I Will Go	31
Chapter Five - What It Could Say	43
Chapter Six - The Kinsman-Redeemer	51
Chapter Seven - The Manipulator	59
Chapter Eight - Boaz at the Crossroads	65
Chapter Nine - The Story of Mr. Ho Suchaone	71
Chapter Ten - What Might Have Been	83
Chapter Eleven - The Book of Ruth?	89
Chapter Twelve - Grandma!	95
Chapter Thirteen - Marvelous Grace	105
Chapter Fourteen - M&M's or Skittles	109
Endnotes	115

Preface

When my daughter, Rebecca, was a little girl, she had the hardest time making up her mind. Often, I would take her into a 7-11 (when we were on the East Coast), or a Circle K (if we were on the West Coast), and tell her to pick out a candy bar. What happened next is the stuff messages are made of.

Becky would stand in front of the candy counter for what the Bible calls the "process of time" - which I think means a long time. While I would never pretend to understand what is going on the in the mind of a little girl, I think she was trying to decide what kind of candy she wanted.

"M&M's - they melt in your mouth; not in your hands. Skittles is real fruit - it must be good for you. Three Musketeers is big on chocolate and low on fat. Nestles Crunch is the official candy bar of the Boston Celtics."

The problem is that these stores are open 24 hours. I could pass a lot of birthdays waiting for Becky to decide if it were going to be M&M's or Skittles. So when either the sun rose the next morning, or my patience wore out, whichever was first, I knew it was time to help out my little girl.

Out came my wristwatch. (If you are not sure what a watch is - Google it.) I would hold it up and start the countdown.

"10, 9, 8 7..."

My daughter would start to panic. A decision had to be made.

"6, 5, 4, 3..."

Now a bead of sweat would cross her forehead. Her little body would begin to tremble.

"3, 2, 1.."

When I hit zero, one of two things would happen. Either Becky would decide between M&M's or Skittles, or I would make the choice for her. One way or another, a decision would be made.

M&M's or Skittles. Little girls need to make choices. So do the rest of us.

Introduction

The mighty military commander of the Old Testament, Joshua, is probably best known for a brief but powerful message that he delivers to the children of Israel. It is easy to hear some exasperation in his voice as he stands before people who seem to rally behind God one day, and then bow to a pagan idol the next day. Maybe an old man of one hundred and ten just doesn't care about being 'politically correct,' nor does he care what opinion polls say.

He lays it on the line:

"And if it seem evil unto you to serve the LORD, choose you this day whom ye will serve; whether the gods which your fathers served that were on the other side of the flood, or the gods of the Amorites, in whose land ye dwell: but as for me and my house, we will serve the LORD." (Joshua 24:15)

It is not just choose - it is choose now! The old warhorse is tired of their games and promises. He is weary of their guarantees. "Either live for Jesus or live for the Devil. Just decide something! And by the way, regardless of what the rest of the world does, we are going to serve the LORD!"

What a message! Today, we are used to ministers who tread lightly. They choose every word carefully so as not to offend. People are pampered and petted to the place where they have no concept of the meaning of living for Christ. Instead of "Lord, what wilt thou have me to do?" (Acts 9:6), people go to a house of religion to tell God, "Here is what you can do for me." The biggest crowds flock to the arena where they are told that God wants them healthy, wealthy, and happy.

The *Book of Ruth* is a fascinating bridge between the chaos that we read about in the *Book of Judges*, and the biographies of Samuel and David that follow in *1 and 2 Samuel*. In the days when the heroes are men like Samson and Jephthah, the testimony and courage of Ruth sets quite the example.

The *Book of Ruth* tells the remarkable story of people at the 'candy counter.' They have to decide if it is going to be *M&M's or Skittles*. The choices they make will determine the course of their life, and they will remind us that our lives are the result of our choices.

It all starts in a rather surprising manner. We might expect the story of Ruth to rise from a spectacular

Introduction

miracle or a mighty moving of God. Instead, the catalyst for her improbable story is a catastrophe. Who would ever think good might come from such words as these?

"Now it came to pass in the days when the judges ruled, that there was a famine in the land" (Ruth 1:1).

Chapter One
A Famine in the Land

God summarizes the book of Judges with these words: "In those days *there was* no king in Israel: every man did *that which was* right in his own eyes" (Judges 21:25). It was a time of disorder and distress. Every chapter in the book of Judges seems to carry the human story to new depths. To be sure, there are occasions where the Lord is able to work in unusual ways, but as Judges progresses, those interventions seem to be the exception rather than the rule.

We should not be surprised. When humans have set themselves and their opinions as the standard of righteousness, morals will quickly disintegrate and then disappear. When our human thinking rules, there is no room for God and His Word.

Somewhere, in the midst of all this confusion, the story of Ruth begins. It may have been as early as the days of Ehud in Judges 3, or as late as the story of Jephthah in Judges 11.[1] The highly reliable *KJV Reese Chronological Study Bible* puts it between Judges 3 and 4.[2] It is a time when the judges are the official rulers, but human hearts are the real authority.

A horrific famine decimates the land of Israel.[3] To the few Israelites who are faithful to Jehovah, and are students of the Bible, this is expected. Long before the story of Ruth, God used His mouthpiece, Moses, to warn the people of the dire consequences of abandoning the Word of God. Deuteronomy 29 lists forty-nine curses God will send, one of which says, "The LORD shall make the rain of thy land powder and dust: from heaven shall it come down upon thee, until thou be destroyed" (Deuteronomy 28:24). Verse 1 reminds us that God keeps His promises.

A man named Elimelech is standing at the 'candy counter.' Ironically, he lives in an insignificant little town called Bethlehem-Judah, which literally means the 'house of bread and praise.' There is no bread in the 'house of bread' because the people are serving themselves. There is no praise in the 'house of praise' because the people are magnifying themselves.

The name Elimelech means "my God is king," suggesting that he grew up with parents of strong conviction who wanted their child to know the Lord.[4] The famine is going to test his personal convictions. He is tempted to move his family to Moab, but he knows it is the home of many idols. There is already enough Bible to testify to the trouble waiting on the other side of that border.[5]

M&M's or Skittles. It is time for Elimelech to make a critical choice. On the one hand, he can choose to stay home in Israel and trust God to meet his needs even in the midst of a famine. He can choose to protect his wife, Naomi, and his boys, Mahlon and Chilion, from the pagan idolatry that dominates the land of Moab. He can decide to learn the lesson from the Bible in Genesis 12. With a famine decimating the land, Father Abraham decided to move his family out of God's land to the pagan country of Egypt. That was a choice Israel would regret for a long, long time.

On the other hand, Elimelech's wallet is screaming at him. There are bills to pay and no money for the bills. It would appear from Ruth 4 that Elimelech has sold off his family plot of land to try to make ends meet. Times are desperate. The pressure is real.

Perhaps there is another clue in Ruth 1:2, where we read that the Elimelech family were "Ephrathites." It is believed the Ephrathites were descendants of the mighty man of God, Caleb, and his wife, Ephrath. Some of their sons were founding fathers of Bethlehem (1 Chronicles 2:19; 2:50-51).

One writer explains it like this:

"If this clan descended from Caleb, the author may have identified this family as Ephrathite to picture it as an aristocratic one - one of the "first families of Bethlehem."

He thereby underscored the humiliating tragedy involved: the Vanderbilts have suddenly become poor sharecroppers."[6]

Finances have a way of pressuring a man. Pride has a way of making it worse.

Mr. Elimelech, it is *M&M's or Skittles*. What do you choose to do?

The Bible says, "And a certain man of Bethlehemjudah went to sojourn in the country of Moab, he, and his wife, and his two sons" (Ruth 1:1). We can imagine the conversation as he travels those fifty miles towards the south and east. "Boys, Moab is a dangerous place for Hebrews. These people have been our enemies for a long time. These are the very people that hired Balaam to curse us! For that reason, God has cursed them!"[7]

It would seem that Elimelech does not intend to stay in Moab for a long time. The Bible says he "went to sojourn," meaning they were intending to reside there temporarily.[8] He does not move to a walled city in Moab, nor to a village, but instead sets up residence in "the country of Moab," meaning the fields and farmlands.

Humans have a way of rationalizing unbiblical decisions. Certainly, Elimelech is not going to tell his wife and sons, "I choose to disregard the Bible. I choose to disobey God's clear command. I choose to reject His warnings." He will not say, "I am making

Chapter One - A Famine in the Land

money the god of our family. I would rather have silver and gold than Jesus."

It sounds a little better when we soothe our consciences by convincing ourselves that our wrong choices are only temporary. "As soon as the famine is over, we are going right back home. When I have paid some bills, then we will be faithful to the Lord again!"

But that is not how it plays out in Moab. "And they came into the country of Moab, and continued there" (Ruth 1:2). Somehow, "sojourn" turns into "continued there." Temporary turns into permanent. A business trip becomes an indefinite period of time.

Then we read these heartbreaking words: "And Elimelech Naomi's husband died" (Ruth 1:3). No cause of death is recorded, and the silence of the Bible leaves many unanswered questions. How did he die? Why did he die? Is he being judged of God? There is nothing but crickets.

There is another point that we may miss, but the reference to Elimelech is somewhat stunning. He is now referred to as "Naomi's husband." Naomi is the leader of this home. She will make the choices. She will rule the roost.

It will be more than a decade before Naomi considers going home to the land of bread and praise, so Moab is the burial place for her husband. This is a choice of shame and judgment. Throughout the Old Testament, godly people follow the example of Joseph who refused to allow his bones to be buried in Egypt. Hebrew men were to be buried in the land that God gave them. It is the man who is being judged by God who dies "in a polluted land" (Amos 7:17).

We may never know all the reasoning Elimelech uses to go to Moab, but his decision to abandon the Bible for finances is a disastrous choice. While he is running away from famine in Bethlehem, he runs right into the clutches and claws of death in Moab. He reminds us that nothing is safer than the Will of God and the Word of God.

A preacher from Tennessee told this story:

There's an old story, a fable, about a rich merchant of Baghdad who had a servant. The servant came to him and said, "Master, I want you to give me one of your best horses: I must flee."

The merchant said to his servant, "Why do you need to flee?"

He said, "I was in the marketplace today and a sinister figure jostled me. When I turned and I looked in his face, I was staring in the face of death. Master, give me a horse. I must flee to Samarra."

The master, loving his servant, said, "Take my best horse, and flee, if you will."

Later that day, the rich merchant of Baghdad went to the marketplace, saw death - this sinister, hooded figure. He said to death, "Death, why did you startle my servant when you saw him?"

Death responded, "I didn't mean to startle your servant. It was your servant that startled me. I didn't expect to see him here, for I have an appointment with him tonight in Samarra."[9]

We will join Elimelech at the candy counter. We have choices to make.

Do I follow my wallet or my Bible? Do I follow my fears or my Heavenly Father? Do I follow my human reasoning or the Will of God?

M&M's or Skittles. It is time to decide. For Elimelech, his choice ends in disaster. The day will come where we will either rue our choices or rejoice in them.

Chapter Two
Crossroads

"And the woman was left of her two sons and her husband" (Ruth 1:5). Life is unraveling for Naomi. After burying her husband in the pagan sands of Moab, she refuses to return home to Bethlehem until the famine is over. Ruth 1:6 may be hinting at the real reason Elimelech left the land of God. Perhaps there is truth in the old adage: "If momma ain't happy, ain't nobody happy."

Life marches on for this little family. Mahlon and Chilion grow up in the country of Moab, and one day they meet young ladies. Mahlon meets a young Moabitess named Ruth. Chilion falls in love with Orpah. The wedding bells ring out, and there is new hope in the heart of Naomi. Perhaps God will bless her with a grandchild.

The days, months, and years pass, but there is no baby. Ten years later, life strikes another cruel blow when Mahlon and Chilion die. Once again, no reason is given, but with the years advancing, time is running out for Naomi. We have all known widows facing severe hardships, but widows in Bible times were especially hopeless and helpless. With no husband, no sons, and no grandsons, Naomi is facing dire circumstances. It would seem she is cursed by God. "The woman was left of her two sons and her husband" (Ruth 1:5). Her life is so miserable, she is only called "the woman." Her family is about to become extinct.

Naomi decides to return to Bethlehem. "She had heard in the country of Moab how that the LORD had visited his people in giving them bread" (Ruth 1:6). Now that the famine is over, it is okay to obey the Bible again. Ruth and Orpah join her as she starts out for home and Judah. They come to the crossroads, and it is time to say goodbye.

"And Naomi said unto her two daughters in law, Go, return each to her mother's house: the LORD deal kindly with you, as ye have dealt with the dead, and with me. The LORD grant you that ye may find rest, each *of you* in the house of her husband" (Ruth 1:8-9). The floodgates are about to open: "Then she kissed them; and they lifted up their voice, and wept." It is an emotional scene as the ladies bid goodbye.

Ruth and Orpah cannot stand to see their mother-in-law in this condition. They will not let her suffer alone. They will make sure she is taken care of. It is

Chapter Two - Crossroads

truly a moment of sacrifice as they tell her, "Surely we will return with thee unto thy people." They will join Naomi in her journey and go to Bethlehem.

Little do they realize that they are about to make the most critical decision of their entire lives. The choice they make in the next five minutes will count for eternity. It is countdown at the crossroads for two ladies.

First, Orpah has a choice to make. She is being yanked in two directions. On the one hand, her emotions are telling her to go to Bethlehem and help Naomi, but on the other hand, her purse is telling her to go back to Moab. Her Bible is telling her to go to Bethlehem, but her future is found in Moab. Bethlehem is the right choice but the difficult choice; Moab is the easy choice but the wrong choice.

It is classic *M&M's or Skittles*. Will Orpah choose Bethlehem or Moab? Will she choose Jehovah or Chemosh, the chief idol of Moab? Will she go the hard way or the easy way? It is neither simple nor easy, but it is a choice that must be made.

So Orpah, what do you choose?

We note that Orpah never makes the wrong choice. She does not begin to sing, "I have decided to follow Satan." She does not shake a fist toward Heaven, grab her purse, run back to Moab, and bow down before the first Chemosh idol she can find. She does not make the wrong choice.

However, we also note that Orpah does not make the right choice. She does not break out into a chorus of *I Have Decided to Follow Jesus*. She is waffling and wavering. Amazingly, she is about to live up to her name.

The name Orpah, (not Oprah),[10] comes from a word referring to the neck or back of an animal.[11] It gives the picture of someone who is constantly looking back, or one who is double-minded.[12] The legend is born. Orpah does not make a wrong choice. Orpah does not make a right choice. Orpah doesn't make any choice. Truly, a "double minded man *is* unstable in all his ways" (James 1:8). *M&M's or Skittles*. This poor lady cannot decide.

Naomi, for all her faults, knows the difficult life of Bethlehem is no place for a confused Orpah. So when Orpah cannot make a decision, Naomi makes one for her:

"And Naomi said, Turn again, my daughters: why will ye go with me? are there yet any more sons in my womb, that they may be your husbands? Turn again, my daughters, go your way; for I am too old to have an husband. If I should say, I have hope, if I should have an husband also to night, and should also bear sons; Would ye tarry for them till they were grown? would ye stay for them from having husbands? nay, my daughters; for it grieveth me much for your sakes that the hand of the LORD is gone out against me." (Ruth 1:11-13)

Chapter Two - Crossroads

It is all so tragic. When Orpah cannot make up her mind, her mother-in-law makes the decisions for her. She will "turn" back from living for the Lord. She will return to her "mother's house".[13] And most tragically, she will go back to the "gods" of Moab. No one prays. No one opens the Scriptures. Naomi has spoken and everyone is expected to dutifully obey.

After a few more tears, Orpah kisses her mother-in-law and heads home to Moab. We can almost visualize her slow walk over a distant hill. She not only disappears from sight, but she also disappears from the pages of Scripture. We never read her name again. *M&M's or Skittles.* She is the woman who can not decide.[14]

Orpah serves as a warning to young people today. Many are not heading in the wrong direction; they are not heading in any direction. A pastor asks a high school senior, "What are your plans? What are you going to do about the Will of God?"

A young man waffles. "I know I should seek God's Word and God's Will, but I don't know what that will cost me. I know I should… I think I want to… ." There is no purpose. There is no conviction. He graduates from high school without a plan. Soon, he gets a job. One day, his co-workers invite him to a sports bar after work. He knows he has no business there, but one of the guys says, "Hey, we know you are religious. You don't have to drink. We are just going to watch a ballgame!"

So he joins them, orders a burger and a coke, and has a good time. A few weeks later, somebody has a birthday. "You can't have a toast with a diet coke! Anyway, what's wrong with one beer?"

One beer becomes two beers. Once a week becomes every day. Soon, another man is hooked on the bottle and may well be on his way to living the horrible life of the drunkard. He is playing a risky game that often destroys the brain, heart, pancreas, mouth, liver, and immune system. He is drinking a poison that steals money, ruins morals, destroys families, and kills innocent people.[15]

It is not that he chose to be a drunk. When he didn't make any choice at all, someone made the choice for him.

M&M's or Skittles.

A young lady is graduating from high school. Her pastors asks, "What are your plans? What are you going to do about the Will of God?"

She is not quite sure. "I know I should… I think I want to… ." She is not a stubborn, rebellious lady who lives to break her parents' hearts. She simply stands at the crossroads of life and fails to make a choice. One day, she meets a man who makes the choices for her. She convinces herself that it will be a fairy tale story. They always live happily ever after on TV. But not this time. A few years later and a few babies later, a young mother has to rear some children because a bum has run out on his family.

We live in an incredible prosperous country full of opportunities, but people by the boatloads still find ways to ruin their lives. How is this possible?

No one ever wakes up in the morning and says, "I think I would like to become a drunk." No one graduates from high school and says, "I think I would like to wind up in jail." No one wakes up on her wedding day and says, "I think I would like to be miserable for the rest of my life." If no one plans to make a mess of his life, then we need to stop and figure out why there are so many disasters.

One of Satan's greatest devices is to convince us to choose tomorrow what should be chosen today. The unsaved man convinces himself that he can repent at the 11th hour, but he dies at 10:30. Convinced by his favorite singers that God is 'there all the time,' the weak Christian keeps promising God what he is going to do 'one day,' but 'one day' never comes. We are not choosing to go to Hell. We are not choosing to live a selfish life. We are not choosing anything.

Time passes on. We abrogate life's choices. We wake up one morning and discover it is too late to make a choice. It has already been made for us.

M&M's or Skittles.

Ronald Reagan had an aunt who took him to a cobbler for a pair of new shoes. The cobbler asked young Reagan, "Do you want square toes or round toes?" Unable to decide, Reagan didn't answer, so the cobbler gave him a few days.

Several days later the cobbler saw Reagan on the street and asked him again what kind of toes he wanted on his shoes. Reagan still couldn't decide, so the shoemaker replied, "Well, come by in a couple of days. Your shoes will be ready." When the future president did so, he found one square-toed and one round-toed shoe. "This will teach you to never let people make decisions for you," the cobbler said to his indecisive customer.

"I learned right then and there," Reagan said later, "if you don't make your own decisions, someone else will."[16]

Orpah stands at the crossroads to make the biggest decision of her life, and without deciding, she ends up in Moab worshipping a vile idol named Chemosh. This is not her choice. This is the result of her not making a choice.

M&M's or Skittles. If we do not decide what we will do with our lives, then we are deciding to let someone else make the choice.

Chapter Three

Going Home

Ruth is watching Orpah walk back towards Moab. Imagine the thoughts swirling through her mind where fear and faith are warring.

Fear says, "Ruth, you better follow Orpah back to Moab. If you go to Bethlehem, you have no chance of getting married. After more than ten years of marriage, you have no children, and you will never have a son unless you go back to Moab. If you head to Bethlehem, you will be dirt poor the rest of your life. You will struggle to eat. You will be reminded every day that you are a Moabitess - you are not one of them.[17] Back to Moab! It is the only choice."

It is a compelling argument. There are not a lot of logical reasons for Ruth to follow Naomi to Bethlehemjudah. Faith does not have much to offer, at least from a human point of view. She is making a decision that is as difficult as Abraham's decision. The difference, of course, is that Abraham had the verbal promise of God that He would "bless" him and make his name "great." There is no record of such a promise to Ruth. She is really walking by faith into a deep, dark hole.

If fear weren't bad enough, Ruth had Naomi doing everything humanly possible to get her to return to Moab. She tells Ruth the only way that she will "find rest" is by returning to the land of Moab. In the language of the Old Testament, the word for "rest" is closely related to word for 'security.' Instead of a life of restlessness and wandering, Ruth can enjoy "peace, permanence, and the satisfaction of having (her) daily needs met."[18]

She reminds Ruth, "I am too old to have an husband" (Ruth 1:12). Naomi was probably pushing fifty years old. In the context of the Old Testament, that is known as a senior citizen. She cannot bear children even if she were to get married. Ruth must know when Naomi dies, she will be alone in a strange land with no one who cares for her. There is only one solution:

"Behold, thy sister in law is gone back unto her people, and unto her gods: return thou after thy sister in law" (Ruth 1:15).

What could possibly motivate Ruth to go to Bethlehemjudah?

Chapter Three - Going Home

When we sit at a computer to write a paragraph, there are many different methods of emphasizing the text and making it jump off the page. <u>We can underline the text.</u> *We can put the text in italics.* **We can make the text bold.** We can change the font of the text. We can change the color of the text. Desktop publishing gives us many options to accentuate a point that were not available in Bible times.

The Bible, by necessity, uses different methods to show emphasis. One of them is repetition. When a word or phrase is repeated in a short space, God is calling attention to it. Looking for repetition is a great method of Bible study. It is one way that God puts the text in italics and makes it bold.

The word "return" is such a word in Ruth 1. In our English Bible, the word is found eight times. The word "turn" is found two more times.[19] In verse 6, Naomi returns from Moab to Bethlehem. In verses 11 and 12, Naomi tells the two ladies to return to Moab. When Ruth refuses, Naomi's language is a little stronger as she tells her to return to her family (verse 15). Then in verse 22, the Bible simply tells us that Naomi "returned" to her home. The word is a drumbeat in the background of the chapter. Everyone is returning somewhere.

After the Bible tells us that Naomi "returned' (Ruth 1:22), the Word of God makes this amazing statement about Ruth: "...and Ruth the Moabitess, her daughter in law, with her, which returned out of the country of

Moab." While it may be easy to roll right past these words, the final appearance of the word "return" in Ruth 1 should stop us in our tracks.

It is not just Naomi who returned to Bethlehem. ***Ruth "returned" as well.***

There is no reason to imagine that Ruth has ever set a footprint in the soil of Judah at any time in her life. Moabites are not welcome there, and they have no desire to go there. There is no remote verse in the Bible suggesting she has ever been to the land of Jehovah. The rendering in the Jewish language makes the point with these words: "Naomi returned, and Ruth the Moabite her daughter-in-law with her, the one returning."[20]

What then is Ruth returning to?

The story of Ruth's people is not a pretty one. It all begins with their ancestral father making a choice. "And Lot lifted up his eyes, and beheld all the plain of Jordan, that it *was* well watered every where, before the LORD destroyed Sodom and Gomorrah, *even* as the garden of the LORD, like the land of Egypt, as thou comest unto Zoar. Then Lot chose him all the plain of Jordan; and Lot journeyed east: and they separated themselves the one from the other" (Genesis 13:10-11).

What a difference between the decision making of Lot and his great, great, great, (etc) granddaughter. Ruth says, "I go where God wants me to go." Lot

Chapter Three - Going Home

says, "I go where my wallet wants me to go." Ruth says, "I will live in God's land." Lot says, "I will live in Satan's land." Ruth says, "I will live with God's people." Lot says, "I will move away from Abraham." The contrasts are both stunning and endless.

Lot is walking the road of disaster. He not only chooses to pitch "his tent toward Sodom" (Genesis 13:12), but he also ultimately decides to move into the city (Genesis 19:1). It goes from bad to worse. Before the sordid story of Genesis 19 concludes, fire and brimstone from Heaven destroys Sodom and many members of Lot's family, his wife dies a horrible death, and in a drunken stupor he molests his two daughters. It is from this horrible wickedness his older daughter bares a son and calls his name Moab.

This is Ruth's history. Lot is Moab's 'George Washington.' Their foundation was not with an idol named Chemosh, but with the living God of Israel. Her ancestry goes all the way back to Genesis 12 where Abram enters the land of Canaan with his wife Sarai and his nephew Lot. In a historical sense, she truly is returning home.

But there is a far more important reason that Ruth comes 'home' to Bethlehem. We don't know the particulars of her testimony, but the day had come in her life where she trusted Jehovah as her Savior. Her nation taught her to follow an idol that could only promise death and misery. She had a ring-side seat to the religion Isaiah described:

"He heweth him down cedars, and taketh the cypress and the oak, which he strengtheneth for himself among the trees of the forest: he planteth an ash, and the rain doth nourish it. Then shall it be for a man to burn: for he will take thereof, and warm himself; yea, he kindleth it, and baketh bread; yea, he maketh a god, and worshippeth it; he maketh it a graven image, and falleth down thereto. He burneth part thereof in the fire; with part thereof he eateth flesh; he roasteth roast, and is satisfied: yea, he warmeth himself, and saith, Aha, I am warm, I have seen the fire: And the residue thereof he maketh a god, even his graven image: he falleth down unto it, and worshippeth it, and prayeth unto it, and saith, Deliver me; for thou art my god. They have not known nor understood: for he hath shut their eyes, that they cannot see; and their hearts, that they cannot understand. And none considereth in his heart, neither is there knowledge nor understanding to say, I have burned part of it in the fire; yea, also I have baked bread upon the coals thereof; I have roasted flesh, and eaten it: and shall I make the residue thereof an abomination? shall I fall down to the stock of a tree? He feedeth on ashes: a deceived heart hath turned him aside, that he cannot deliver his soul, nor say, Is there not a lie in my right hand?" (Isaiah 44:14-20)

But one day, Jehovah captures her heart and her life is transformed. Everyone can see her faith in her Savior and her willingness to live for Him. It is Boaz who puts it like this:

"It hath fully been shewed me, all that thou hast done unto thy mother in law since the death of thine husband: and how thou hast left thy father and thy mother, and the land

Chapter Three - Going Home

of thy nativity, and art come unto a people which thou knewest not heretofore. The LORD recompense thy work, and a full reward be given thee of the LORD God of Israel, under whose wings thou art come to trust." (Ruth 2:11-12)

Ruth is abiding 'under His wings!' God is like a mother bird stretching her wings over Ruth and protecting her every step. Under His wings is a safe place; a place of provision; a place of refuge; a warm place. There is no place better than 'under His wings.'

We can almost hear her singing:

Under His wings I am safely abiding,
Though the night deepens and tempests are wild,
Still I can trust Him; I know He will keep me,
He has redeemed me, and I am His child.

Under His wings, under His wings,
Who from His love can sever?
Under His wings my soul shall abide,
Safely abide forever.[21]

Ruth is coming home!

Years ago, William Kirkpatrick was leading the music for a camp meeting near Philadelphia. God had given him reason to doubt the salvation of a certain soloist that had been chosen to help with the meeting. Each night, after singing his solo, the man would leave, never staying to listen to the message or participate in the fellowship of God's people. Feeling burdened for this singer, Mr. Kirkpatrick began to pray for the working of the Holy Spirit in his heart.

Two days went by, and although the messages of the evangelists were stirring many hearts, the singer failed to be moved. As Mr. Kirkpatrick continued to pray he questioned, "Will God ever hear my prayers?"

He was so burdened that he felt the Lord led him to perform a rather unusual plan. The Lord led him to write a special invitation song with the soloist in mind, and then have him sing it. He did this, and that very evening, the Lord worked. The soloist, instead of leaving directly as was his custom, stayed for the preaching and was the first at the altar to accept Christ as Savior.

I've wandered far away from God,
Now I'm coming home;
The paths of sin too long I've trod,
Lord, I'm coming home.

I've wasted many precious years,
Now I'm coming home;
I now repent with bitter tears,
Lord, I'm coming home.

I'm tired of sin and straying, Lord,
Now I'm coming home;
I'll trust Thy love, believe Thy word,
Lord, I'm coming home.

My soul is sick, my heart is sore,
Now I'm coming home;
My strength renew, my home restore,
Lord, I'm coming home.

My only hope, my only plea,
Now I'm coming home;
That Jesus died, and died for me,
Lord, I'm coming home.

I need His cleansing blood I know,
Now I'm coming home;
Oh, wash me whiter than the snow,
Lord, I'm coming home.

Coming home, coming home,
Nevermore to roam;
Open wide Thine arms of love,
Lord, I'm coming home.[22]

Ruth is tired of Chemosh. Ruth is tired of Moab. Ruth is tired of idols. Ruth is tired of sin.

M&M's or Skittles. Ruth is going home.

Chapter Four

I Will Go

M&M's or Skittles. Ruth is standing at the crossroads between Bethlehem and Moab, and she must decide. She will either go the easy way but the wrong way back to Moab, or she will go the hard way but the right way to Bethlehem. She will either bow her knee to Jehovah or to Chemosh.

Naomi is not helping. She is telling Ruth to go back to Moab, back to her family, and back to her pagan idols. She paints such a dreary picture of hopelessness that no one would ever want to follow God.

It is a signature moment in the Bible that seems to come out of nowhere. All of her world is telling Ruth to follow Orpah back to Moab, but the Bible says, "Ruth clave unto (Naomi)" (Ruth 1:15). In the Hebrew language of the Bible, the noun form of the word 'cleave' is the word that is used for glue.[23] She is sticking to Naomi, and no one can pry her loose!

The word 'cleave' is also an interesting word in our language. It is what the English professors would refer to as a 'Janus' word - a word which is its own opposite. Cleave can mean to split apart, and it can mean to stick together. Orpah is cleaving from Naomi and leaving for home. Ruth is cleaving to Naomi and won't be shaken loose.

Naomi tries again: "Behold, thy sister in law is gone back unto her people, and unto her gods: return thou after thy sister in law." It is the fourth time that Naomi tells Ruth to leave her and go back to Moab. Ruth has heard enough.

What follows is the first time Ruth ever speaks in the Bible. It is a bit like the three Hebrew boys in Daniel 3 - Hananiah, Mishael, and Azariah. They only speak one time in all the Bible, but their words are for the ages. "If it be *so*, our God whom we serve is able to deliver us from the burning fiery furnace, and he will deliver *us* out of thine hand, O king. But if not, be it known unto thee, O king, that we will not serve thy gods, nor worship the golden image which thou hast set up" (Daniel 3:17-18).

So it is in Ruth 1:16. Ruth does not say a lot, but when she speaks, it is compelling and courageous. She begins: "Intreat me not to leave thee, *or* to return from following after thee." She is fed up with Naomi's orders so now she has some orders for her! Her language is a "straightforward and strong command telling Naomi to back off."[24] She is refusing

Chapter Four - I Will Go

to obey the unbiblical orders of her mother-in-law. She is telling her to 'knock it off!'

The next thirty-seven words will set the direction for the rest of her life. There will be no turning back from this decision. These words will either bring regret or rejoicing, but it is Ruth's 'Rubicon.' She can never go back.

> *"...for whither thou goest, I will go;*
> *and where thou lodgest, I will lodge:*
> *thy people shall be my people,*
> *and thy God my God:*
> *Where thou diest, will I die,*
> *and there will I be buried..."*

It takes her about seven seconds to make five choices.

Choice #1 - I Will Go Where God Wants Me to Go
"...for whither thou goest, I will go..."

Ruth tells Naomi that she is willing to go anywhere in the Will of God. There are no restrictions or exceptions. By now, she must know that the road to Bethlehem offers her no promises nor guarantees, yet, she will not be stopped. Her feet are already moving to the land of her God. The word for "go" and 'walk' is the same.

Jewish rabbis living in Old Testament times claimed that Ruth was responding to Naomi's diatribe. Trying to convince Ruth to return to Moab, she tells her that she does not want to come to Bethlehem because "we are commanded to keep the Sabbaths and holidays, not to walk more than two thousand cubits." We can almost hear her say, "You don't want to live in Bethlehem. You cannot even walk where you want on the Sabbath!"[25]

Ruth replies, "Whither thou goest, I will go."

It is what the spirit God is looking for from His people. I fear that most Christians are not interested in allowing God to fill out the itinerary for their lives. They will go where God wants them to go until that means they have to go to church on Sunday night. They will go where God wants them to go until they learn that God does not want His people visiting Satan's playgrounds. They will go where God wants them to go so long as their schedule is not interrupted.

While preaching at Open Door Baptist Church in Summit, Mississippi, I once met an 80 year old man who was asked to give his testimony. He said, "I was living the comfortable life of a retired man in Hattiesburg, when at the age of 60, I knew the Lord was calling me to the mission field. It was a little surprising that He would call a Southern boy to Siberia, but that is what He did!"

He went on to describe his work with a missionary in that Russian wasteland. He talked about baptismal services where they literally took chainsaws and cut holes in the ice. There were, of course, hardships beyond our comprehension, but then he told us, "I wouldn't trade my time in Russia for anything else in the world! It was the time of my life!"

When we choose the Will of God, we are telling God that He gets to tell us where we are going to go for the rest of our lives.

Choice #2 - I Will Live Where God Wants Me to Live
"...and where thou lodgest, I will lodge..."

If the Jewish teachers are to be believed, Naomi is explaining to Ruth that living as a Jew means "we are commanded not to spend the night together with non-Jews."[26] God expects His people to not only live differently than the world, but He also expects them to lodge differently. Pagan people have a different family culture than righteous people.

Ruth responds, "And where thou lodgest, I will lodge." It is a most interesting word in the language of the Bible. "Lodge" normally speaks of temporary housing,[27] much like we would speak of spending a night in a hotel room. Ruth is saying that she may never have a permanent home, but it doesn't matter. Perhaps she is humming: *"A tent or a cottage; why should I care? They are building a palace for me over there!"*

When we choose to live where God wants us to live, we are telling Him to make our accommodations.

Choice #3 - God's People Will Be My People
"...thy people shall be my people..."

When the italics are removed, the verse looks like this: "thy people - my people." The simplicity is powerful! When one is putting their life on the altar of sacrifice, it does not take a dictionary to understand what they are saying. One does not need a lawyer to parse the words. "Thy people - My people!"

Ruth is making a clean break. In the rear-view mirror is the land of Moab with its abundance of idols. She knows that her choice to go to Bethlehem means that she has a new people in her life. Even though the Bethlehemites, to put it kindly, would be very slow to accept her, she is accepting them. "God's people are now my people. The crowd I once called my own are no more my people. God has changed my relationships."

It is the story of the man transformed by the Gospel. Before he was saved, he ran with the world, smoked with the world, played with the world, joked with the world, cussed with the world, and flat-out lived for the world. But trusting Christ completely transforms the man. Now he would rather go to church on Sunday than go to the party on Saturday. Now he would rather sing "To God be the Glory" than go to a jam-packed arena to 'rock out.' Now he would rather enjoy the 'water of the Word' than the newest brew. His friends don't know what happened!

Pastor Peter explains it perfectly:

"For the time past of our life may suffice us to have wrought the will of the Gentiles, when we walked in lasciviousness, lusts, excess of wine, revellings, banquetings, and abominable idolatries: Wherein they think it strange that ye run not with them to the same excess of riot, speaking evil of you..." (1 Peter 4:3-4).

They call him 'strange.' They would call Ruth 'strange.' 'Strange' is how the world describes a new creature in Christ.

The Jewish rabbis claim that Naomi is telling Ruth, "We are commanded to keep six hundred thirteen commandments."[28] She needs to know that living in Bethlehem will transform her lifestyle, but it is precisely what Ruth wants. Ruth is more than happy to follow the standards and convictions God demands from His people.

I remember graduating from a public high school excited about going to Bible college. I had enough of the language, attitude, filthiness, and wickedness on display in the hallways. I heard enough mocking of the Bible from teachers. I was going to a Bible school where they did not laugh at God in class - they prayed to Him. Instead of hearing Him cursed, I was going to a place where He was praised. In the dorms there would be prayer meetings instead of parties.

I couldn't wait to go. The rules didn't bother me - I wanted them. Twelve years in Satan's playground was enough. "Thy people - my people."

Choice #4 - The God of the Bible Will Be My God
"...and thy God my God..."

What words are these words! Ruth has witnessed "the hand of the LORD (that) is gone out against (Naomi)." We might think that most humans would abandon such a God. He is certainly not the God of the modern house of religion who exists to 'give me what I want.' Most humans would call the God of Ruth 1 a harsh God.

Consider:

- *God allows Elimelech to die*
- *God allows Mahlon to die*
- *God allows Chilion to die*
- *God does not bless Naomi with grandchildren*
- *God seems to be allowing the family to become extinct*

Who in the word would ever want this God to be his God?

Ruth raises her hand and says, "I do."

"Your God - My God!"

Chapter Four - I Will Go

Ruth didn't need the sloppy religion of our day. She didn't need a minister telling her that Jesus will make you happy, healthy, wealthy, and victorious. Her brand of salvation is not a selfish, me-first religion that fixes all my problems. She has a front row seat to the judgment of God upon a backsliding family, yet, she is all in. She compares the Living God of the Bible with the pagan idol Chemosh, and she is more than willing to join Job in saying, "Though he slay me, yet will I trust in him" (Job 3:15).

The Jewish historians claim that Ruth was responding to a most important command given to Israel: "Thou shalt have no other gods before me...thou shalt not make unto thee any graven image..." (Exodus 20:3-4). We can hear Naomi trying to dissuade Ruth by saying, "Bethlehem is different from Moab. We don't have idols of gold like your family has. Idols in Israel don't work!"

It is exactly what Ruth is looking for. In a story we will have to wait for Heaven to hear, she had placed her trust in Jehovah. She is now abiding under the shadow of His wings, and she has no interest in the pagan idols that could do nothing but make her a child of Hell.

"Your God - My God!" It is all Ruth wants.

Choice #5 - I Will Die Where God Wants Me to Die
...Where thou diest, will I die, and there will I be buried...

Ruth's decision is not an emotional trip to the altar at the conclusion of a preaching service. It is the choice of a lifetime. Ruth looks at a woman perhaps twenty years her senior, and tells her that long after she is gone, Ruth will still be serving God. One day, Ruth is going to be buried in the sands of Israel too.

We may miss the significance of the reference to burial, but Naomi surely did not. The place of burial was incredibly important in Bible times. The great story of Joseph concludes with these words: "God will surely visit you, and ye shall carry up my bones from hence" (Genesis 50:25). Joseph is making it crystal clear to his family. "You will not bury me in Egypt because I do not belong to Egypt. I don't care how long it takes, you make sure these bones are buried in the Promised Land!"

Centuries later, God delivers the people from the oppression of Pharaoh. As Moses leads them towards the Red Sea, the Bible says, "Moses took the bones of Joseph with him" (Exodus 13:19). It is not until Joshua 24:32 that the Bible puts a wrap on Joseph's life: "And the bones of Joseph, which the children of Israel brought up out of Egypt, buried they in Shechem, in a parcel of ground which Jacob bought of the sons of Hamor."

When Ruth tells Naomi that she will be buried in Bethlehem, she is saying that she has a new family. She cares nothing for the custom that says she belongs in a family tomb in Moab. Tradition said that families were expected to remain united even after death, but this will not work for Ruth. She will be buried right alongside Naomi, because she has a new people and a new family. This is for the rest of her life and beyond.

It would be hard to imagine this moving movement in the Bible becoming even more dramatic, but Ruth finds a way. She makes five incredibly powerful statements that demand 'her soul, her life, her all,' yet, she is going to take things to an even higher level.

Ruth takes a solemn oath:

"...the LORD do so to me, and more also, if ought but death part thee and me."

It is a formula that we read in eleven other Old Testament Scriptures.[29] It is a serious moment that we would have to see to appreciate.

She begins by calling out the name of Jehovah, her personal God and Savior. In her past, Ruth may well have called upon the name of Chemosh, but this is not the past. She will make her oath before Him.

It is very possible that Ruth's oath includes some gestures, such as the crossing of a hand across the throat - the slitting of the throat. Ruth is promising to live for her God, and should she fail in her promise, she is asking God to "do so" to her. That "do so" is not described with words but with gestures.[30]

Standing at the crossroads, Ruth is willing and ready to decide. There is no waffling for her. She raises her hand to her God and surrenders the rest of her life to Him. "For to me to live *is* Christ, and to die *is* gain" (Philippians 1:21).

When James Calvert went out as a missionary to the cannibals of the Fiji Islands, the captain of the ship that carried him there sought to turn him back by saying, "You will lose your life and the lives of those with you if you go among such savages." Calvert's short reply said it all: "We died before we came here."[31]

M&M's or Skittles. Orpah stands at the crossroads and can not decide. Ruth stands at the crossroads and is ready to make her choice.

What will we do with our lives?

Chapter Five

What It Could Say

Ruth and Orpah are standing in the same place, on the same day, with the same opportunity, but their paths will presumably never intersect again. Orpah chooses to return to her home in Moab, while Ruth chooses to return to her home in Bethlehem (even though she had never yet been there).

Orpah kisses her mother-in-law and is on her way back to her family and her gods. We never hear from her again. For all we know, she may have become a great and famous woman in the land of Moab, but in the Bible, the silence is deafening. Her choice to make no choice leaves us shaking our heads and wondering, "What could have been?"

The Bible, of course, has a lot to say about Ruth. The eighth book in our Bible is called the *Book of Ruth*, and it is the only book in the Old Testament named after a non-Israelite. There are other foreign women in the Old Testament who play significant roles, but there is no *Book of Zipporah* or *Book of Rahab*. She joins Esther in a title role of the most significant work in human history. It is impossible to estimate the number of Bibles in existence, but it is in the billions., and every one tells the story of Ruth. For every person in the last fifty years who has read a story of Harry Potter, there are at least ten who have read the story of Ruth.[32]

When one remembers that the *Book of Ruth* was acted out in the form of a play in Old Testament times, the Ruth story would have to go down in history as one of the most read, most known, most beloved stories ever.

A pastor of yesteryear told this story:

When Benjamin Franklin was the United States Ambassador to France, he became a member of a French literary society, an organization that gathered to tell their favorite stories. One day, Dr. Franklin took the story of the 'Book of Ruth' and rewrote it in his own words. Then he stood up and read the story to this French literary society. When he finished reading, they said, "Dr. Franklin, that is the greatest love story written in any language, and this society requests that you would give us permission to put it in printed form and distribute it for worldwide distribution, that other people might enjoy the romance and the love story that you've written." Now Ben Franklin had pulled a trick on them. He stood up and he said, "I'm sorry, but it has already been printed and it has already been given to the world. You'll find the story that I have just read in the Bible, the book you profess to despise, but whose content apparently you know very little about."[33]

How does Ruth go from an insignificant foreigner to a beloved woman of great esteem? Believe it or not, it all 'happened.'

The glorious decision of Ruth 1:16 meets an empty stomach in Ruth 2:2. She is hungry and tells Naomi, "Let me now go to the field, and glean ears of corn after *him* in whose sight I shall find grace." Off she goes to 'the field.'

In Bethlehem, there was one massive field where people did their farming. The city was not surrounded by many farms as we might see in rural America, but rather, one great field was divided into family plots. There would be nothing more than a line of stones dividing the field.

Ruth goes out to "glean ears of corn," which is very different from reaping ears of corn. After the workers reaped the harvest, the law of God allowed foreigners, orphans, and widows to gather the scraps and leftovers that were missed or left behind. Even for the most destitute, God expected them to labor and eat by the sweat of their brow.

It must seem that the whole world is against Ruth. She is going to the field by herself - Naomi has no interest in helping. We are reminded again in verse 2 that she is "Ruth the Moabitess." The chances of someone wanting to help a foreigner are between slim and none. She is a widow who was married for more than ten years and never had a son. Now, she is hungry.

Hungry. Hopeless. Helpless.

When she heads to the field that morning, she knows her only hope is someone, anyone, in "whose sight I shall find grace." Ruth is very vulnerable. Someone needs to show favor to her.

Then it 'happened.' The Bible puts it like this: "and her hap was to light on a part of the field *belonging* unto Boaz" (Ruth 2:3). It is one of the great words in the Bible.

The word "hap" refers to a "chance event; a happening; fate."[34] In the midst of the patchwork of properties in that massive field, she 'happens' on the plot owned by Boaz, who 'happens' to be a relative of the Elimelech family. It 'happens' to be the season of barley harvest (1:22) when the boss would frequent the field to keep an eye on his business. And of course, Boaz 'happens' to come out from the city. A lot 'happens!'

The world calls this 'luck,' but we know it as 'God making it happen.'

This remarkable story culminates in Ruth 4:13, where Boaz marries Ruth. "When he went in unto her, the LORD gave her conception, and she bare a son."

Chapter Five - What It Could Say

The boy is named Obed. One day Obed has a son named Jesse. One day Jesse has a son named David. We know him as David the champion over Goliath. We know him as David the "sweet psalmist of Israel" (2 Samuel 23:1). We know him as David the man "after (God's) own heart" (1 Samuel 13:14). We know him as King David.

He was Ruth's great-grandson. It all 'happened.'

Then there is the little matter of Matthew chapter 1. The dominant word in the first chapter of the New Testament is easily the word "begat." " Abraham begat Isaac; and Isaac begat Jacob; and Jacob begat Judas..." (Matthew 1:2). It is tempting to skip such verses of repetition in the Bible, but doing so means one misses great blessings. One such blessing is found in Matthew 1:5:

> *"And Salmon begat Booz of Rachab;*
> *and Booz begat Obed of Ruth;*
> *and Obed begat Jesse..."*

Imagine that! 1300 years later, God is still reminding us about this Moabitess woman!

Add another 2000 years to that number and we are still talking about this special lady. This coming Sunday, her story will be told in countless Sunday School classes, and her courage will be the theme of sermons declared from pulpits. She will bless and encourage the hearts of men and ladies in Bible studies and personal study. This Sunday, like last

Sunday, Ruth's story will be heard around the world.

But there is another part of her story that rises to a higher level. It culminates in Luke 2:1-7:

"And it came to pass in those days, that there went out a decree from Caesar Augustus, that all the world should be taxed. (And this taxing was first made when Cyrenius was governor of Syria.) And all went to be taxed, every one into his own city. And Joseph also went up from Galilee, out of the city of Nazareth, into Judaea, unto the city of David, which is called Bethlehem; (because he was of the house and lineage of David:) To be taxed with Mary his espoused wife, being great with child. And so it was, that, while they were there, the days were accomplished that she should be delivered. And she brought forth her firstborn son, and wrapped him in swaddling clothes, and laid him in a manger; because there was no room for them in the inn."

When one traces all the 'begats' of Matthew 1, he learns that Ruth's great, great, great….great grandson was this same Joseph, the husband of Mary. And if that is not enough, it all 'happens' at Bethlehem. Sure enough, the same place where Ruth 'happens' to land on the part of the field owned by Boaz, is the same place where the King of Kings and Lord of Lords is born!

It is more than amazing! Ruth the Moabitess is the great, great, great…great grandmother, on His human side, of the Lord Jesus Christ. It all just 'happened.'

Chapter Five - What It Could Say

Consider this list:

- The *Book of Ruth* is one of sixty-six books in the Bible
- The story of Ruth is one of the most beloved story in world history
- Ruth's great grandson is mighty King David
- Ruth is mentioned in the New Testament
- Ruth's story is still known around the world
- Ruth is an ancestor of the Lord Jesus Christ

Now stop and ask yourself this question. How easily could the list read like this:

- The *Book of Orpah* is one of sixty-six books in the Bible
- The story of Orpah is one of the most beloved story in world history
- Orpah's great grandson is mighty King David
- Orpah is mentioned in the New Testament
- Orpah's story is still known around the world
- Orpah is an ancestor of the Lord Jesus Christ

So why does the list say 'Ruth' and not 'Orpah?' The answer is simple. When Ruth stands at the crossroad, she says, "For whither thou goest, I will go; and where thou lodgest, I will lodge: thy people *shall be* my people, and thy God my God: Where thou diest, will I die, and there will I be buried."

When Orpah stands at the exact same crossroad, she says:

M&M's or Skittles.

No choice is the wrong choice!

Chapter Six
The Kinsman-Redeemer

Ruth 'happens' to land on the field belonging to Boaz. Boaz 'happens' to come to the field when she is there. The rest, as they say, is history.

Before we actually meet Boaz, we are told that he is a relative of Elimelech, a mighty man (which may indicate a military background), and a wealthy man. We picture an influential man with a powerful presence. In the city of Bethlehem, he is a 'somebody.'

There is something else about Boaz that Hollywood and the children's story books ignore. The man is not just old, he is *very* old.

The Reese Chronological Study Bible provides this timeline:

- Boaz born in 1421 BC (Salmon would have been 54 years old; Rahab 50 years old)

- Ruth born in 1329 BC
- Ruth and Naomi go to Bethlehem in 1299 BC
- Ruth marries Boaz who is 122 years old in 1299 BC[35]

While precise dating in the Old Testament is often an inexact science, there is no way to get from Salmon to David without Boaz being a very senior citizen (Matthew 1:5). The words of ancient Jewish sages, while not the same as the inspired Word of God, can offer historical insights to Bible events. They claim that Boaz passed away the very night that Obed was conceived. If nothing else, this would give a plausible explanation for the fact that he is nowhere to be found after Ruth 4:13.[36]

As long as we are on the contributions of the wise men of Israel, there are a few other interesting claims they make about Boaz. They say that he had many children from a previous marriage and had attempted "120 engagements and weddings for his children, but they all died in his lifetime."[37] If this is true, Boaz is facing the end of his life without a family to carry on his name. It is also claimed that Boaz's wife died the day that Ruth entered Bethlehem, explaining the crowd that met Naomi.[38]

It can be hard to separate the fact from the fiction, but there is no mistake in admiring the character of this faithful man. The first time he speaks in the Bible,[39] he says to the common laborers:,"The LORD *be* with you" (Ruth 2:4). The normal greeting would

Chapter Six - The Kinsman-Redeemer

be a simple 'shalom,' but Boaz seems to have a vested interest in the spiritual condition of his reapers. Their response, "The LORD bless thee," indicate a respect beyond the norm for workers and their master.

Although there are a lot of reasons to love Boaz, one stands above all others. From the moment he first appears in the Bible with his workers, he reminds us of the Lord Jesus Christ. He is a magnificent 'type' of Christ.

Here is my partial list of the many ways Boaz reminds us of the Savior:

- *Boaz is from Bethlehem*
- *Boaz is a kinsman redeemer*
- *Boaz is a mighty man*
- *Boaz is rich*
- *Boaz loves the common man*
- *Boaz gives the gift of grace*
- *Boaz extends 'unmerited favor'*
- *Boaz knows Ruth before she knows him*
- *Boaz is a friendly comforter*
- *Boaz dips the sop*
- *Boaz satisfies*
- *Boaz gives over and above*
- *Boaz gives the message: 'Fear Not'*
- *Boaz purchases Ruth*
- *Boaz takes his bride*

Yet, even for Boaz, there is that *M&M's or Skittles* moment. It is such a bizarre and strange moment in the Bible, we often pretend like it is not there and gloss over it. Still, Ruth chapter 3 is as much inspired Bible as John chapter 3.

To set up the moment, we take a look at chapter 2. Boaz comes to the field, greets his workers, and instantly notices Ruth. She is so out of place, Boaz does not ask, "Who is she?" Instead, the question is: "Whose damsel *is* this?" (Ruth 2:5) It is a logical question given the setting. Surrounded by servants, she would appear to be another servant girl.[40] She must belong to someone.

The superintendent identifies her as Ruth the Moabitess, and explains that she has come seeking permission to glean the sheaves after the reapers.[41] Instead of brashly claiming her rights under the law, this humble lady says, "I pray you, let me glean and gather after the reapers among the sheaves" (Ruth 2:7). Such grace in Ruth prompts great grace from Boaz, who responds in a demonstrative fashion. He tells Ruth in no uncertain terms that she is not to glean elsewhere, but she is to "abide here fast by my maidens" (Ruth 2:8).[42]

Boaz assures the safety of Ruth, and then tells her, "And when thou art athirst, go unto the vessels, and drink of *that* which the young men have drawn" (Ruth 2:9). In the culture of Bethlehem, where the foreigners would draw water for the Israelites and the women would draw water for the men, Boaz is inviting Ruth to drink of his workers' supply. Such an invitation is extraordinary. The ever appreciative Ruth can only bow to the ground and say, "Why have I found grace in thine eyes, that thou shouldest take knowledge of me, seeing I *am* a stranger?" (Ruth 2:10).

Ruth needs grace. Ruth finds grace. It is an 'amazing' grace when a mighty man like Boaz recognizes a "stranger" like Ruth, yet the most 'amazing' aspect of grace is that the giving never stops. Ruth, the insignificant Moabitess, the 'stranger' to Bethlehem, is about to hear words that must have floored her:

"It hath fully been shewed me, all that thou hast done unto thy mother in law since the death of thine husband: and how thou hast left thy father and thy mother, and the land of thy nativity, and art come unto a people which thou knewest not heretofore. The LORD recompense thy work, and a full reward be given thee of the LORD God of Israel, under whose wings thou art come to trust." (Ruth 2:11-12)

Long before Boaz meets Ruth, Boaz knows Ruth! She will love him because he first loves her!

"It hath fully been shewed me." It is the language of an inquisitive man. He knows her whole story. He knows about Ruth standing at the crossroads. He knows she loves Jehovah, the God of Israel. He knows of her great compassion towards an unappreciative mother-in-law. He knows her willingness to lay it all on the altar of sacrifice. He knows her desire to live a life of faith. He knows her testimony. He knows and admires this 'Ruth the Moabitess.'

Boaz is not finished. Next, he invites Ruth to join his reapers for lunch, an invitation that surprises everyone. The appetizer is bread dipped in a sauce, the main course is roasted corn, and Ruth eats until she is "sufficed." It is more than enough.

Still, the man of grace is not done giving. When Ruth leaves, he tells the workers to let her glean the good stuff instead of the leftovers. Then he issues a stern warning telling them to keep their hands off. "Reproach her not...rebuke her not" (Ruth 2:15-16) gives us a sense of the danger a woman like Ruth faces in the fields at harvest time. There is drinking. There is money. There is immorality. Boaz wants every worker to know that Ruth is not to be taken advantage of.

And then there are the "handfuls of purpose" (Ruth 2:16) Boaz leaves for her. The gleaners normally cut the grain with the right hand and hold the sheaves in their left hand. Some of the handfuls of grain were to be purposely left behind for Ruth, making her job all the easier. She goes home that evening with an "ephah of barley" (Ruth 2:17). There is some question as to the exact measurement of an ephah in that day, but it is somewhere between thirty to fifty of our pounds.[43] It is five times more than she and Naomi would need.[44]

Chapter Six - The Kinsman-Redeemer

When Naomi hears that Boaz is the provider, she finally admits, "The man *is* near of kin unto us, one of our next kinsmen" (Ruth 2:20). Unbeknownst to Ruth, there is kin living in Bethlehem.

Boaz is not just a relative, he is a kinsman. The full understanding of such a man is that he is a 'kinsman-redeemer.' His responsibilities come into play upon the death of a father/husband when there are no sons to care for the family. With the death of Elimelech, Mahlon, and Chilion hanging over the story, the kinsman-redeemer needs to step up and save the family.

The Old Testament has strict orders for a kinsman-redeemer:

1. If a family is forced to sell their land in times of economic hardship, the kinsman-redeemer is to repurchase the land and return it to the original owner.
2. If any family members are forced to sell themselves as slaves, the kinsman-redeemer is to repurchase the humans and set them free.
3. The kinsman-redeemer has the responsibility of avenging the murder of a family member.
4. The kinsman-redeemer is to receive monies paid for restitution for a wrong against a deceased family member.
5. The kinsman-redeemer is to assist family members in lawsuits brought against them.[45]

We can not help but conclude that all of this is a stunning revelation for Ruth. How is it possible that Naomi hides this from her? What kind of woman plays the helpless widow card and sends an innocent foreigner to dangerous fields? What possesses her to return home crying that she is "empty," when there is able kin to take care of her?

Naomi's actions in Ruth 2 are despicable, but they will get even worse in chapter three.

Chapter Seven

The Manipulator

In September of 2018, the eastern seaboard of the United States was ravaged by Hurricane Florence. When the storm made landfall in North Carolina, The Weather Channel sent Mike Seidel and a crew to report. The cameras show Mr. Seidel struggling to maintain his balance as the winds are blowing. It is an 'end of the world' drama as the intrepid reporter tells those who are not as brave as he, "This is about as nasty as it's been."[46]

Then the camera crew inadvertently caught two men casually strolling down the road. When Mr. Seidel and his bosses offered a flimsy and silly reason for the false reporting, America could only laugh. Once again, the fake news media members had exposed themselves as master manipulators of the news. We cannot even get an honest weather report.

There are serious problems with people who are continually manipulating others. Psychologists define them as attempting "the exercise of undue influence through mental distortion and emotional exploitation, with the intention to seize power, control, benefits, and privileges at the victim's expense."[47] These psychologists would have a field day with Naomi.

Naomi's relationship with Ruth is a strange one. In chapter one, she tries to control Ruth's life and make choices for her, and when Ruth rebukes her, she refuses to speak to her. In chapter two, she sends Ruth out alone to a very dangerous place without warning. The chapter concludes by informing us that Naomi is duplicitous all along. She is a master manipulator using Ruth at every turn.

In chapter 3, Naomi is at it again:

"My daughter, shall I not seek rest for thee, that it may be well with thee? And now is not Boaz of our kindred, with whose maidens thou wast? Behold, he winnoweth barley to night in the threshingfloor. Wash thyself therefore, and anoint thee, and put thy raiment upon thee, and get thee down to the floor: but make not thyself known unto the man, until he shall have done eating and drinking. And it shall be, when he lieth down, that thou shalt mark the place where he shall lie, and thou shalt go in, and uncover his feet, and lay thee down; and he will tell thee what thou shalt do." (Ruth 3:1-4)

Chapter Seven - The Manipulator

Naomi begins with a series of rhetorical questions. She begins by claiming to have Ruth's best interests at heart: "My daughter, shall I not seek rest for thee, that it may be well with thee?" There is something phony in these words. Yesterday, Naomi was willing to send Ruth to a dangerous setting without warning. Today, she pretends that she is only concerned about her wellbeing. The appropriate word would be 'disingenuous.'

Then she tells Ruth that Boaz is one "of our kindred." This little piece of information was conveniently left out of the famous 'woe is me' speech of Ruth 1:11-13. She knows at harvest time that Boaz will be found in the threshingfloor winnowing the barley. After the harvest is cut and gathered, it will be carried to the hard rock surfaces on hilltops. When the winds are blowing, the product will be tossed in the air by means of a fork with large teeth. The heavier kernels of grain will fall to the floor while the winds blow the excess away. The evening breezes are much easier to deal with than the gusty winds of the daytime, so night time is the preferred time to winnow.[48] There is no doubt that Boaz will be there. At winnowing time, the men will sleep at the threshingfloors to guard the fruits of their labor against thieves or animals.[49]

"Wash thyself therefore, and anoint thee, and put thy raiment upon thee." Ruth will not be going to the fields to work. Naomi has something else in mind. In another Old Testament text, the actions of verse 3 are associated with seduction.⁵⁰

Next, Naomi tells Ruth to "get thee down to the floor." She will go that night. Many writers have tried to absolve Naomi of any questionable motives or actions, but no one can explain why she has to go that night. What is the big hurry? What has to be done under the cover of darkness that cannot wait until the morning? What has to be done tonight that cannot wait until next week?

The harvest season brings out many unsavory characters, for there is plenty of food, plenty of money, and plenty of booze.⁵¹ "At winnowing time the threshing floor often became a place of illicit sexual behavior. Realizing that the men would spend the night in the fields near the piles of grain, prostitutes would go out to them and offer their services."⁵² Boaz, realizing the potential scandal of the nighttime visit, would later tell Ruth: "Let it not be known that a woman came into the floor" (Ruth 1:14).

Naomi tells Ruth to hide herself from Boaz until the right moment. "Make not thyself known unto the man, until he shall have done eating and drinking." The secrecy and deception add to the suggestiveness of the night.

Naomi finishes her scheme with these words: "And it shall be, when he lieth down, that thou shalt mark the place where he shall lie, and thou shalt go in, and uncover his feet, and lay thee down; and he will tell thee what thou shalt do." These words are loaded with sexual overtones.

The Hebrew word for "lieth down," found eight times in this chapter,[53] is used in the sordid stories of Lot and his daughters, David and Bathsheba, and Amnon and Tamar. The word "uncover" refers to illicit sex in multiple Old Testament passages.[54] While uncovering "the feet" seems innocent enough in our culture, (though a bit strange), in Bible times, it had a suggestive meaning.[55] The phrase "lay thee down" is similar to the English expression 'to sleep with someone.'[56]

Like a politician, Naomi puts in a layer of plausible deniability. Standing alone, any single one of her orders would seem to be harmless enough, but when one adds them up, the sum is not pretty. At best, Naomi is urging Ruth to act disgracefully.

Perhaps there is another motive at play. The constant reminder that Ruth is a 'Moabitess' recalls the racial attitudes she deals with on a daily basis since her arrival in Bethlehem. It may be a reminder of the Moabites' origins in Genesis 19, or the disgusting account of Numbers 25, or even the actions of Tamar in Genesis 38. Naomi's lack of respect for Ruth in the first two chapters only magnify the issue. Ruth is to do what it takes to gain the favor and services of Boaz. Naomi has it all figured out. The manipulator has spoken.

So Ruth says, "All that thou sayest unto me I will do."

Chapter Eight
Boaz at the Crossroads

"And she went down unto the floor, and did according to all that her mother in law bade her" (Ruth 3:6). "Bade" is the root of the word meaning commandment.[57] Naomi issues her orders, and Ruth is going to obey them to the letter.

Boaz enjoys his meal and returns to a "heap of corn" to find a comfortable place to sleep. It may seem a little strange to our 'select comfort' way of thinking, but most of the world prefers a hard mattress.

Ruth comes in "softly," uncovers "his feet," and lays next to him (Ruth 3:7). That is all she does. She does not have to flirt. She does not have to seduce. She does not have to sexually degrade herself to get something from a man. Although Naomi words are full of suggestive behavior, Ruth manages to do them without compromising her purity or Boaz's reputation. Ruth will never go to that level because she is a "virtuous woman" (Ruth 3:11).

A virtuous woman is a woman of noble character.[58] A virtuous woman is a strong woman.[59] A virtuous woman is a worthy woman. A virtuous woman is a good woman.[60] A virtuous woman is a Proverbs 31 woman:

"Who can find a virtuous woman? for her price is far above rubies. The heart of her husband doth safely trust in her, so that he shall have no need of spoil. She will do him good and not evil all the days of her life. She seeketh wool, and flax, and worketh willingly with her hands. She is like the merchants' ships; she bringeth her food from afar. She riseth also while it is yet night, and giveth meat to her household, and a portion to her maidens. She considereth a field, and buyeth it: with the fruit of her hands she planteth a vineyard. She girdeth her loins with strength, and strengtheneth her arms. She perceiveth that her merchandise is good: her candle goeth not out by night. She layeth her hands to the spindle, and her hands hold the distaff. She stretcheth out her hand to the poor; yea, she reacheth forth her hands to the needy. She is not afraid of the snow for her household: for all her household are clothed with scarlet. She maketh herself coverings of tapestry; her clothing is silk and purple. Her husband is known in the gates, when he sitteth among the elders of the land. She maketh fine linen, and selleth it; and delivereth girdles unto the merchant. Strength and honour are her clothing; and she shall rejoice in time to come. She openeth her mouth with wisdom; and in her tongue is the law of kindness. She

looketh well to the ways of her household, and eateth not the bread of idleness. Her children arise up, and call her blessed; her husband also, and he praiseth her. Many daughters have done virtuously, but thou excellest them all. Favour is deceitful, and beauty is vain: but a woman that feareth the LORD, she shall be praised. Give her of the fruit of her hands; and let her own works praise her in the gates."

Our pagan culture mocks a virtuous woman, but a man like Boaz admires her.

It is midnight, and he awakens to find a woman at his feet.[61] When one remembers this story takes place in the days "when the judges ruled," he might expect that most men would welcome such a visit, but Boaz is not going to do what is right "in his own eyes." He will leave those actions for Samson.

With a strange woman lying at his feet, the Bible says, "The man was afraid" (Ruth 3:8). What a great response! He is afraid of losing his testimony! He is afraid of dishonoring his body! He is afraid of displeasing his God! Fear is his instinctive reaction.

Instead of thinking he can get away with it, or assuming that no one will ever know, Boaz knows that "the eyes of the LORD *are* in every place, beholding the evil and the good" (Proverbs 15:3). What a wonderful testimony! He is afraid because he is a virtuous man!

So the virtuous woman meets the virtuous man. Such a story is not welcome in our Hollywood cesspools, but the man with a love for Christ, and the woman with a heart for the Will of God, can rest confident in His matchmaking skills. Virtuous men and women don't need the help of unsaved people and their websites.

Now this amazing story is about to take an unexpected turn. "And he said, Who *art* thou? And she answered, I *am* Ruth thine handmaid: spread therefore thy skirt over thine handmaid; for thou *art* a near kinsman" (Ruth 3:9). The Hebrew word for "skirt" is the same word we read as "wings" in Ruth 2:12: "The LORD recompense thy work, and a full reward be given thee of the LORD God of Israel, under whose wings thou art come to trust."

A lost, pagan Moabitess had turned from her dead idols of religion to the living Savior of Israel. As God stretched out His wings to protect and secure her soul, she is going to ask Boaz to stretch out his skirt to protect and secure her physical life. As she has learned to trust Jehovah for eternity, she is willing to trust Boaz for today. As she came to her Lord with nothing to offer, she approaches Boaz as a simple "handmaid" - a slave girl.

In verse four, Naomi tells Ruth, "He will tell thee what thou shalt do." Ruth is taking no chances. She is not going to wait for Boaz to figure it out. She lays it on the line: "Thou *art* a near kinsman."

Chapter Eight - Boaz at the Crossroads

Ruth is telling Boaz in no uncertain terms that he is responsible for repurchasing the land Elimelech sold. It is his duty to be the redeemer. Boaz finds himself at the crossroads with a choice to make. On the one hand, the Word of God, which is the law of the land, commands him to care for Naomi and Ruth. On the other hand, there are plenty of human excuses for Boaz to shun these duties, not the least of which is his old age.

M&M's or Skittles. It is the midnight hour for Boaz, and it is the time to make a choice. He may be an old man, but old men still have to choose 'whom they will serve.' Choices are not just for teenagers.

Boaz steps to the plate and knocks it out of the park.

"And now, my daughter, fear not; I will do to thee all that thou requirest" (Ruth 3:11). Note the words "to thee." This is not simply an honorable man fulfilling an obligation of the law of God, or a generous man extending charity to a destitute family. What Boaz is going to do, he is going to do for Ruth. In an astounding turn of events, Boaz is going to take the place of the servant. This "mighty man of wealth" is going to meet the needs of this "Moabitess" woman. He may even give us a tiny glimpse of the One who "though he was rich, yet for your sakes he became poor, that ye through his poverty might be rich" (2 Corinthians 8:9).

M&M's or Skittles. Even an old man has to make the right choices.

Chapter Nine
The Story of Mr. Ho Suchaone

In his book *Begat*, David Crystal, a highly respected British linguist, lists two hundred fifty-seven expressions and idioms that the King James Bible has given to our English language. Though other writers might count some he ignores, every linguist would have to agree with his conclusion: "No other single source has provided the language with so many idiomatic expressions."[62] William Shakespeare comes in a distant second with less than one hundred such contributions.

One of our expressions comes from Ecclesiastes 10:1: "Dead flies cause the ointment of the apothecary to send forth a stinking savour." A 'fly in the ointment' is something or someone that ruins an otherwise perfect or pleasant situation.

For Ruth, the 'fly in the ointment' sounds like this: "Howbeit there is a kinsman nearer than I" (Ruth

3:12). It is an 'uh-oh' moment for Ruth. She must have thought, "If it sounds too good to be true, it probably is."

The sterling integrity of Boaz manifests itself again. He freely tells Ruth there is another man in Bethlehem who is a closer relative of Naomi, and as such, he has first dibs on the land. Boaz is so refreshing. If God is in it, he won't need to pull strings, finagle outcomes, and 'lawyer up.' Once again, he reminds us of the Lord Jesus: "Neither was guile found in his mouth" (1 Peter 2:22).

It is a moment of irony for Naomi. In Ruth 1:21, she bitterly moans that no one is there to aid her. Now, it would seem she has more helpers than she needs!

The Bible tells us with nine simple words that the night passes: "And she lay at his feet until the morning" (Ruth 3:14). Those nine words must seem like eternity for Ruth. Before the sun rises the next morning, Ruth slips away with "six measures of barley," a load that will cover a lot of breakfasts.[63] She tells Naomi what happened that night, and then says, "These six *measures* of barley gave he me; for he said to me, Go not empty unto thy mother in law" (Ruth 3:17). We should note this is the final time that Ruth speaks in the Bible.

Naomi recognizes that the waiting game will soon be over. "The man will not be in rest, until he have finished the thing this day" (Ruth 3:18).

Chapter Nine - The Story of Mr. Ho Suchaone

The morning takes us to the city gate of Bethlehem. The gate, of course, is the main entrance into the city, but in Bible times, it is also the hub of the city. People greet each other and spread the latest news. Children meet their friends and play. The old guys sit around and say a lot while really saying nothing. In colonial America, it was called the 'town square.' Today, we call it McDonalds.

The city gate is also the place for formal assemblies. Often, the Bible refers to kings sitting in the gate and addressing the people. Judges would sit at the gate and pass sentence. Businessmen would cut deals at the gate. Poor people would look for handouts at the gate. "The gate was the normal place for public business, and specifically for the kind of business described in this chapter."[64]

"Then went Boaz up to the gate, and sat him down there: and, behold, the kinsman of whom Boaz spake came by" (Ruth 4:1). It is the fifth time we read the word "behold" in the *Book of Ruth*, a word that "expresses strong feelings, surprise, hope, (and) expectation."[65] Of all people, who shows up at the city gate but the man who is the nearer kinsman! Who could have expected that?

By now, we shouldn't be surprised at all the 'coincidences' in the story of Ruth. She is not lucky. Behind the scenes, God is making it happen.

Boaz greets the gentleman with these words:

"Ho, such a one! turn aside, sit down here."

"Ho, such a one!" The English professor would call this an indefinite pronoun. It is used in Bible times when an author does not want to mention a specific person or place.[66] Similar language is used in two other Old Testament verses where there is a deliberate attempt to dismiss true identity.[67]

Obviously, Boaz knows the man's name. He is a respected leader in the city of Bethlehem, and the rightful redeemer of the founding family of the city. Although the man is certainly Mr. Somebody, God chooses to disregard him in the eternal Word of God. The phrase, "Ho such a one," serves to "diminish our respect for him."[68] As far as God is concerned, *Mr. Somebody* is really *Mr. Nobody*. He is *Mr. Ho Suchaone!*

But there is more. In the Hebrew language of the Old Testament, the phrase *"Ho such a one"* reads like this: "Peloni almoni." These rhyming words create a wordplay the English teachers call a 'farrago,' a series of meaningless rhymes that produce an idiom. Some examples of English farragos are words like 'helter-skelter,' 'hodge-podge,' and 'hocus-pocus.'[69]

In other words, God not only dismisses the man, but He also disrespects him. The citizens of Bethlehem must see him as a businessman, a successful man, and even an honored man, but *"the LORD seeth* not as man seeth; for man looketh on the outward appearance, but the LORD looketh on the

Chapter Nine - The Story of Mr. Ho Suchaone

heart" (1 Samuel 16:7). God is not impressed with the man's bank account nor with the impressive titles. To God, the man is simply Mr. Ho Suchaone. He is 'Peloni Almoni.'

Boaz gathers ten elders as witnesses (4:2) who will serve as a quorum for the business at hand. It is interesting to watch Boaz operate. Perhaps it is his military background that gives him the gravitas to 'take' ten men from their busy schedules and tell them to sit down. As he speaks, we cannot help but be impressed by the clarity and order of his words. By the time he is done, a great crowd of people will join the proceedings. The man and his bearing demand respect.

Boaz begins with the issue of the land. It appears that Elimelech, facing the burden of the intense famine, was forced to sell the family's plot of ground. Property rights of the Old Testament assured the land would always belong to the original family. They could repurchase the land, or they could wait for the *Year of Jubilee*, at which time the land would be returned to them. When the Bible tells us that Naomi was selling "a parcel of land," it likely means she is giving the authority to use the land to her redeemer. The redeemer will buy back the land and farm it.

Boaz says to Mr. Ho Suchaone, "Buy *it* before the inhabitants, and before the elders of my people. If thou wilt redeem *it*, redeem *it*: but if thou wilt not redeem *it*, *then* tell me, that I may know: for *there is* none to redeem *it* beside thee; and I *am* after thee" (Ruth 4:4). It is a great deal for Mr. Ho Suchaone. Not only will he get a valuable plot of land which should provide a decent financial return, but he will also come out 'smelling like a rose' as the man who cares for the destitute widow. It is a win-win proposition. He quickly responds, "I will redeem *it*."

Imagine Ruth watching all of this. Mr. Ho Suchaone is her closest relative, yet he has done nothing to help her or Naomi. The whole city knows the Naomi story (Ruth 1:19), but this nearest of kin is conspicuous by his absence. When the man says, "I will redeem it," Ruth must have been crushed.

There is still the matter of the 'fine print,' so Boaz continues: "What day thou buyest the field of the hand of Naomi, thou must buy *it* also of Ruth the Moabitess, the wife of the dead, to raise up the name of the dead upon his inheritance" (Ruth 4:5). Boaz is saying to Mr. Ho Suchaone, "If you are going to redeem the land, then you are morally obliged to redeem the lady. You will need to bring her into your family and give her a child to carry on the family name. It is your responsibility according to the law of God!"[70]

We should notice how Boaz refers to Ruth. He reminds Mr. Ho Suchaone that she is Ruth 'the Moabitess.' In the *Book of Ruth*, the constant reminder that Ruth is from Moab serves to help us realize the incredible difficulties she is facing. In the city of

Chapter Nine - The Story of Mr. Ho Suchaone

Bethlehem, there is a built in racism and distrust for all things Moab, and it seems that Boaz is playing on the prejudices of Brother Ho Suchaone. With the reminder that Ruth is the Moabitess woman, the man cannot help but recoil at the idea of Moabitess blood mingling with his family.

So this Mr. Ho Suchaone, aka Peloni Almoni, is having an *M&M's or Skittles* moment of his own. "If I redeem the land then I have to redeem the lady. I will make a lot of money but I will have to live with a Moabitess. I know the right thing to do is help the widow, but what will that do to my reputation?"

M&M's or Skittles. It is time for the man to decide. All of the eyes of the city are upon him. The witnesses are waiting for his response. Boaz is standing right in front of him. The correct description is 'palpable!'

"I cannot redeem" (Ruth 4:6).

What a response! He does not say, "I will not redeem." He says, "I cannot redeem."

When we read the entire verse, the statement is even stronger. "And the kinsman said, I cannot redeem *it* for myself, lest I mar mine own inheritance: redeem thou my right to thyself; for I cannot redeem *it*." The repetition of the statement is a Bible way of showing great emphasis. The words "myself" and "thyself" add to the intensity of the moment.

We must stop and recognize what the man is admitting. He is obligated by the Word of God, which for Israel was the law of the land, to redeem this woman. In effect, Mr. Ho Suchaone is saying, "I cannot obey the Bible. I cannot honor God. I cannot do the right thing."

He is deceiving himself. Of course he can do the right thing and obey the Word of God. No one is holding a knife to his throat. He is using the wrong phrase. He says, "I cannot." He should be saying, "I will not."

Mr. Ho Suchaone is so human! We are so ready to convince ourselves that we 'cannot' obey the Word of God. The pressures are too great and the problems are too intense. So we talk ourselves into believing "I cannot," when the truth is simply: "I will not."

We can always do right before God. We can always stay in God's Word. We can always pray. We can always make His local church our priority. We can always honor Him. It is never an issue of "cannot." If we make wrong choices, it is always a case of 'will not.'

If nothing else, we must appreciate the honesty of Mr. Ho Suchaone. The text gives us the two reasons he is willing to abandon the commands of Scripture. First, he will not redeem Ruth because he loves himself. The phrase "for myself" highlights the great "contrast between the man and Boaz, who appears

Chapter Nine - The Story of Mr. Ho Suchaone

throughout to be operating in the interests of others."[71] This Moabitess damsel is simply going to get in the way of his plans.

Secondly, he is unwilling to "mar" (a word meaning to ruin or destroy) his inheritance. He begins to think, "If I buy Naomi's property, I will lose my investment when this half-Moabitess child of Ruth grows up. More than that, I will have to spend a lot of many taking care of her and her child. This child may even take part of my inheritance that will belong to my real children!" All of a sudden, it is no longer a good deal for Mr. Ho Suchaone. It is going to cost more than it is worth. "No deal!"

Self and Stuff! "I cannot obey the Bible because it is not what I want. I cannot obey the Bible because I am going to lose my stuff." It is the language of the Christian living for the wrong priorities. It is the same old story of the man who is willing to take the free gift of Salvation, and then refuse to live for the Savior.

No wonder the Bible is loaded with verses calling us to make a choice. "Choose you this day whom ye will serve!" We will either choose to live for the offers and pleasures this world can give, or we will choose to seek "first the Kingdom of God." We either live to please ourselves, or we live for the "good, and acceptable, and perfect, will of God." We choose to amass the treasures this world offers, or we choose to "lay up ... treasures in heaven." We can live for self and stuff, or we can live for Christ and eternity, but we cannot live for both.

For twelve seasons, Bobby Richardson played second base for the New York Yankees. He was an exceptional ballplayer who is best known for being named the Most Valuable Player of the 1960 World Series. Bobby was selected for the American League All-Star team eight times. His teams, which included famous players such as Mickey Mantle, Yogi Berra, and Roger Maris, won three world championships.

More importantly, Bobby Richardson was a faithful Christian. We are used to athletes talking about religion, but Bobby Richardson was real. His testimony for Christ was known in and out of the Yankee clubhouse.

In his biography, *Impact Player*, he tells this story:

When my son Robby was a boy, he liked to gather my fan mail from the Yankee Stadium clubhouse and open and read the letters on our way home after games. On one of those rides home, as we were crossing the George Washington Bridge, one particular letter grabbed his attention. "Hey, Dad," he said, "I've got to read this one to you." It was from a man named Walt Huntley, who said he attended a church in Toronto, Canada. He had written a poem that he wanted to give to me because I was a Christian. The title was *God's Hall of Fame*. Robby read Huntley's poem to me as I drove. "Boy," I told Robby,

Chapter Nine - The Story of Mr. Ho Suchaone

"that is good." When we arrived home, I went through the poem again, and as I read and absorbed the words, their meaning rang so true. I liked that poem so much that I knew it was something I wanted to use at my speaking engagements. I had no idea how many times and for how many years I would be requested to recite *God's Hall of Fame*. I have adapted the poem a little over time. It goes like this:

Your name may not appear down here
In this world's Hall of Fame.
In fact, you may be so unknown
That no one knows your name.

The Oscars and the praise of men
May never come your way.
But don't forget - God has rewards
That He'll hand out some day.

This Hall of Fame is only good
As long as time shall be.
But keep in mind, God's Hall of Fame
Is for eternity.

To have your name inscribed up there
Is greater more by far
Than all the praise and all the fame
Of any man-made star.

This crowd on earth, they soon forget
When you're not at the top.

They cheer like mad until you fall
And then the praises stop.

But God - He never does forget.
And in His Hall of Fame,
By just believing on His Son
Forever there's your name.

I tell you, friend, I wouldn't trade
My name, however small,
That's written there beyond the stars
In that celestial hall

For every famous name on earth
Or glory that it shares.
I'd rather be an unknown here
And have my name up there.[72]

So Mr. Ho Suchaone, you are standing at the crossroads. Is it *M&M's or Skittles*? In the *Book of Ruth*, we watch a double-minded lady waffle back and forth, ultimately making no choice. We see a widow raise her hand to her God and surrender her life, counting the cost for Him. Now we witness Mr. Ho Suchaone choosing self and stuff over the Word of God. He has made his choice, but make no mistake, there are consequences for this 'Peloni Almoni!'

Chapter Ten
What Mighty Have Been?

In 1856, the famous American poet, John Greenleaf Whittier, wrote a poem entitled *Maud Muller*. He tells the story of the fateful day when a humble farm girl meets an up and coming judge. They enjoy each other's company, and dream of spending their lives together, but ultimately they go in separate directions. The judge marries a "wife of richest dower, who lives for fashion." As for the young lady, "she wedded a man unlearned and poor…(until) care and sorrow, and childbirth pain, left their traces on heart and brain." The two spend their lives ruing the choices they made.

Mr. Whittier sums up their misery with these words:

For all sad words of tongue and pen,
The saddest are these, 'It might have been'.[73]

It is time for Mr. Ho Suchaone and Boaz to seal the deal. In our day, we have contracts with multiple pages. We sign our names until the ink runs dry. Some old-timers remember the day when a 'man's word was his bond,' and an old-fashioned handshake said it all.

In the days 'when the judges ruled,' contracts were done a little differently. "Now this *was the manner* in former time in Israel concerning redeeming and concerning changing, for to confirm all things; a man plucked off his shoe, and gave *it* to his neighbour: and this *was* a testimony in Israel" (Ruth 4:7). When property was exchanged, a man would hand over his shoe. Should a man try to renege on his word, the shoe would testify against him.

For Mr. Ho Suchaone, it is such a casual statement. "So he drew off his shoe" (Ruth 4:8). He is releasing himself from his Biblical obligation to care for Ruth and her property, and he is publicly giving that 'privilege' to Boaz. Both of the men want the same thing. Boaz wants Ruth to be his wife. Mr. Ho Suchaone wants Ruth to be Boaz's wife.

We cannot help but wonder what Mr. Ho Suchaone is thinking. Certainly, he must walk away happy that all he lost was a shoe. We can almost hear him say, "That was close! I almost lost my inheritance, but instead, I only lost a cheap sandal! I almost had a Moabitess in my family!" I suspect he leaves thinking that he is the winner in this exchange.

But thirty-three hundred years gives us ample time to judge the 'winner' in this story. We look at Boaz and see one of the greatest pictures of Christ in the Bible. We love and admire this man of grace and strength. The people of Israel respected him so much, that when the Temple of Solomon was finally built in Jerusalem, one of the pillars was actually named 'Boaz' (2 Chronicles 3:17).

As for Mr. Ho Suchaone, we don't even know his real name. The Lord takes great pains to make sure we see him as one of the great nobodies in the Bible. When all is said and done, the man lost a lot more than his shoe. He is the classic example as to what "might have been."

He *might have been* the husband of Ruth. "So Boaz took Ruth, and she was his wife" (Ruth 4:13). How easily those words could read: "So Mr. Ho Suchaone took Ruth, and she was his wife." He had the first opportunity to be the human savior of one of the greatest women in world history.

He *might have* had a son named Obed. "And the women her neighbours gave it a name, saying, There is a son born to Naomi; and they called his name Obed" (Ruth 4:17). God intervenes in human affairs again, and a child is born of Ruth and Boaz. It reminds us of the miracle birth of Abraham in his old age, and it foreshadows the birth of John the Baptist from the seed of ancient Zacharias. His name means the "one who serves."[74] He is the miracle baby given of God to care for Naomi in her old age. We will find his name listed in Matthew and Luke. He is in both the royal lineage and the legal lineage of Christ.

He *might have* had a grandson named Jesse. Six centuries later, the mighty prophet Isaiah would write these words: "And there shall come forth a rod out of the stem of Jesse, and a Branch shall grow out of his roots" (Isaiah 11:1). The prophecy of the coming Messiah is a reminder that the humble roots of Jesse not only produced the greatest king of Israel, but also the King of Kings. Seven hundred years later, the Apostle Paul reminds those of us who are Gentiles: "There shall be a root of Jesse, and he that shall rise to reign over the Gentiles; in him shall the Gentiles trust" (Romans 15:12).

He *might have* had a great grandson named David. The final words of the *Book of Ruth* simply say, "Jesse begat David" (Ruth 4:22). When the ladies of Bethlehem hold a little baby in their arms and wish "that his name may be famous in Israel," the certainly did not dream of this. David joins Abraham, Moses, and Elijah as the greatest of Israel's heroes.

Most importantly, he *might have* had a line to the Messiah, the Lord Jesus Christ!

> *"And Jesus himself began to be about thirty years of age,*
> *..being (as was supposed) the son of Joseph*
> *...which was the son of David*
> *...which was the son of Jesse,*

Chapter Ten - What Might Have Been?

...which was the son of Obed
...which was the son of Abraham
...which was the son of Noe
...which was the son of Adam,
which was the son of God."
(Luke 2:23-38)

Buried in the middle of this genealogy, we find these words:

"...which was the son of Booz (Boaz)..."

It could have read; it ***should*** have read:

...which was the son of Mr. Ho Suchaone...

John Phillips wrote this of Mr. Ho Suchaone:

"He did not want to mar his inheritance by marrying a Moabite and putting Moabite blood into his bloodline. He was afraid of the curse of the law. He was afraid, too, that by contaminating the purity of his bloodline, he might render it impossible for one of his sons to be the promised Messiah."[75]

As it turns out, his disobedience to the Bible costs him the opportunity to be in the lineage of the promised Messiah. He thinks he is the winner. He turns out to be a loser.

And we don't even know the man's real name!

For all sad words of tongue and pen,
The saddest are these, 'It might have been'.

Chapter Eleven

The Book of Ruth?

We all love the story of Ruth. We admire her conviction, her courage, and her willingness to surrender to God and His will. Faithfulness, virtue, compassion, and so many other qualities leap out from these pages. With good reason, she is one of the most beloved women in world history.

It is quite stunning, then, when we stop to realize that Ruth is not the main character in the *Book of Ruth*. She certainly has the title role, but there is another story that is given far more importance than the Ruth story. The *Book of Ruth* begins with Naomi, and it ends with Naomi.

Daniel Block took the time to run the numbers:

- Fifty-five of the eighty-five verses in Ruth contain dialogue.

- 678 of the 1294 words in Ruth come from the lips of the characters.
- Ruth speaks less than Naomi and Boaz.
- Ruth's speeches are much shorter than Naomi and Boaz.[76]

If the title were based on the plot line, it would be called *The Book of Naomi*. If it were based on the dialogue, it would be called *The Book of Boaz*. If it were on the importance of genealogy, it might even be called *The Book of Obed*.

When we stop to see the story from Naomi's point of view, an entirely different message comes into focus. There is a heart-breaking moment when Naomi returns to the city of Bethlehem, and the entire city is emotionally "moved" at their return (Ruth 1:19). As the crowd circles around them, they wonder, "Is this Naomi?" It would appear that the years of backsliding have taken their toll. Perhaps she looks much older than she actually is, for the words indicate she is almost unrecognizable to them. Truly, "the way of the transgressor is hard" (Proverbs 13:15).

At just the right moment, Naomi launches into her speech. It is a horrible moment in Bible history. She makes some of the most vicious, angry, and unwarranted charges against God ever recorded. The poison and venom spewing from her soul certainly startle the citizens of Bethlehem, just as they shock us today. Naomi has been holding it all inside, and when the volcano finally erupts, it is Almighty God bearing the brunt of her assault.

"Call me not Naomi, call me Mara: for the Almighty hath dealt very bitterly with me. I went out full, and the LORD hath brought me home again empty: why then call ye me Naomi, seeing the LORD hath testified against me, and the Almighty hath afflicted me?" (Ruth 1:20-21).

Like a lawyer in the courtroom, Naomi is laying out her charges against God. God is a bully. God is unfair. God is cruel. God is unjust. God is afflicting her. She is not simply bemoaning her misery and anguish, she is blaming God for it all, and she is doing so publicly. It is the big story in the book of Ruth that transcends every other narrative. The character of God is challenged! How will God respond?

It is easy for us to look at Naomi and ask, "What are you talking about? You have violated the commands of the Bible at every turn. Now that life has turned sour, how dare you blame God for your miserable condition?"

The list of Naomi's transgressions and offenses are numerous, to say the least. When studying the Bible, it is quite enlightening to track various characters and their traits. When we make a list of the Naomi story in the Bible, it is mighty hard to cast any aspersions at God. He is not to blame for the choices she makes:

1. Naomi and her husband abandon Bethlehem because of a famine in the land.
2. Naomi and her husband willfully disobey the clear command of the Bible in moving to Moab.
3. Naomi refuses to return to Bethlehem upon the death of her husband, so he is buried in a pagan land.
4. Naomi willfully disobeys the Bible in marrying her sons to Moabitess women.
5. Naomi spends ten more years in Moab in disobedience to the Bible.
6. Naomi decides to return home - not because she loves the Lord - but because the famine appears to be over.
7. Naomi sends Orpah back to Moab and its idols.
8. Naomi's invoking the name of Jehovah in pressuring her daughters to worship idols is blasphemous.
9. Naomi uses great pressure to force Ruth back to Moab and its gods.
10. Naomi will not even speak to Ruth after she decides to live for the Will of God.
11. Naomi allows bitterness to consume her life.
12. Naomi blasphemes God again with wicked and vicious charges.
13. Naomi forces Ruth to glean alone.
14. Naomi allows Ruth to provide for her, even though she has multiple kinsmen in the city.
15. Naomi knowingly sends Ruth to a very dangerous place without warning.
16. Naomi sends Ruth out to seduce Boaz.
17. Naomi advises Ruth to behave like a harlot.

Naomi disregards multiple commands from the Scriptures, and when her life hits a brick wall, she has the audacity to indict God. God did not tell Naomi to move to Moab. God did not tell Naomi to stay in Moab. God did not tell Naomi to bury her husband there. God did not tell Naomi to marry her boys to pagans. In fact, in the pages of Scripture, God repeatedly tells her just the opposite!

With the people of Bethlehem for her audience, she launches her tirade against Heaven. God is at fault for all her bitterness and misery and pain. She went out so "full," and now God has made her "empty." She used to be so 'satisfied and happy,' but now she is 'empty-handed and destitute.' He is the reason for the name change from Naomi to Mara. Her life was once lovely and pleasant, but now it is miserable and bitter. And it is all God's fault.

We notice that she does not launch her attacks at God personally. Instead, she attacks Him indirectly through the citizenry of Bethlehem. Her words are selfish and egotistical:

*"Call **me** not Naomi, call **me** Mara: for the Almighty hath dealt very bitterly with **me**. I went out full, and the LORD hath brought **me** home again empty: why then call ye **me** Naomi, seeing the LORD hath testified against **me**, and the Almighty hath afflicted **me**?"*

We watch Naomi ruin her life and cast the blame at God. God is a bully. God is unfair. God is cruel. God is unjust. God is afflicting her. The disasters of her life have nothing to do with her choices or her actions. It is all on God.

She is stubborn. She is arrogant. She is hateful. She is vindictive. She is wrong.

She is so much like me.

Chapter Twelve

Grandma!

For all of the great storylines in Ruth, this is the big one. Naomi is challenging the very character of God. His compassion, His faithful love, and His justice are being called into question. What is God going to do?

Will He rain fire and brimstone from heaven upon her as He did to the cities of Sodom and Gomorrah? Will He send a series of plagues as He did to the stubborn Pharaoh of Egypt? Will He open the ground and swallow her up as He did with the rebellion of Korah? How is God going to respond to these accusations?

In chapter two, Ruth heads to the field to glean after the reapers. It is a long day of gathering barley, but Boaz makes sure there are "handfuls of purpose" for her. As the evening approaches, she takes a stick to beat the grain from the barley, then takes it home to Naomi. It is far more than they need for their daily bread. "Blessed *be* he of the LORD, who hath not left off his kindness to the living and to the dead" (Ruth 2:20). Naomi knows Who put dinner on the table that night.

The story is similar in chapter three. When Ruth returns a second time to her mother-in-law, she is carrying six measures of barley in her veil. Boaz tells her, "Go not empty unto thy mother in law" (Ruth 3:17). The God who allegedly brought her home 'empty' is sure filling up the shelves with food, and He is doing it in a hurry. One might even say that He is giving "good measure, pressed down, and shaken together, and running over" (Luke 6:38).

The giving is only starting. For Naomi, the last nine verses of Ruth are better than Christmas morning.

Ruth 4:13 is a wedding announcement and a birth announcement rolled into one verse: "So Boaz took Ruth, and she was his wife: and when he went in unto her, the LORD gave her conception, and she bare a son." We cannot help but notice the unusual wording. After ten years of marriage to Mahlon, Ruth has no children. We would understand if she had begun to worry that she was barren and unable to have a child. A man as ancient as Boaz is not about to father a child. They are going to need some help.

I love the way an old Jewish teacher put it: "Ruth did her part; Boaz did his part; now the Holy One

Chapter Twelve - Grandma!

said, 'I will do my part.'"[77] My, did God ever do His part!

It is at this moment in Ruth where we find an astonishing aberration. It is the last scene of this amazing play, but Ruth and Boaz are nowhere to be found. The claim of Jewish historians that Boaz died the night the baby was conceived would explain the reason he disappears from the story. But what of Ruth? Why is she suddenly missing in action?

It is all about the 'big story.' Naomi makes her charges, and God is going to answer them. The boatload of barley is just the opening act. Now, in the pages of Scripture, Ruth is going to step aside, and Naomi is going to witness firsthand this God who has "dealt very bitterly with me." The final scene is God and Naomi.

It reads like this:

"And the women said unto Naomi, Blessed be the LORD, which hath not left thee this day without a kinsman, that his name may be famous in Israel. And he shall be unto thee a restorer of thy life, and a nourisher of thine old age: for thy daughter in law, which loveth thee, which is better to thee than seven sons, hath born him. And Naomi took the child, and laid it in her bosom, and became nurse unto it. And the women her neighbours gave it a name, saying, There is a son born to Naomi; and they called his name Obed: he is the father of Jesse, the father of David."
(Ruth 4:14-17)

Naomi will unwrap six magnificent gifts:

The LORD gives her a grandchild! Obed is not just a baby, he is a miracle baby. Standing at the crossroads, a distraught Naomi bitterly proclaims there are no children in her womb (Ruth 1:11). But now, she is holding in her arms the blessing of a most impossible story. She lost her husband, she lost her boys, and she comes home to Bethlehem empty, but God, this same God who has "dealt very bitterly with me," has just done the impossible.

Note the words in Ruth 4:14: "Blessed *be* the LORD, which hath not left thee this day without a kinsman." We would expect the ladies of Bethlehem to say, "Blessed be the LORD, which hath given thee a kinsman." But they use a strange sequence of words when they say, "...which hath not left thee this day without a kinsman." They are clearly recalling the bitter wail of Naomi, and now they are calling her out on this. Naomi says, "God has abandoned me!" The ladies say, "He has not left thee!"

The LORD gives her a kinsman redeemer! This is not just a grandchild, he is called a "kinsman." This is the first and only time in the Bible where a kinsman is someone other than an adult.[78] This statement is unusual for another reason. Most of the time, the name of a child is given before his life's purpose is stated.[79] The fact that the women call Obed a redeemer before we even know his name emphasizes

Chapter Twelve - Grandma!

the great reason he is born. Boaz is the redeemer of Ruth, but Obed is Naomi's redeemer.

The LORD gives her recognition and fame! The ladies' wish for Obed is that "his name may be famous in Israel." Little did they imagine how famous his name would become. Little did they know of a boy named David, or a manger in Bethlehem. They hope he will be famous in Israel, but his story is known around the world!

The LORD gives her a restored life! Babies have a way of doing that. Put a little one in the arms of an old codger and watch everything change. In Ruth 1, the self-centeredness of Naomi is on display. It is all about 'me.' Now, she has a brand new life. There are diapers to change and a little mouth to feed. She will see the first steps, hear the first words, watch the first little tooth come, and relish all the great joys of motherhood. Naomi has something to live for!

In Ruth 1, the story of Naomi is the story of death. There is the death of Elimelech, the death of Mahlon, the death of Chilion, and the impending death of an entire family. But in Ruth 4, there is life everywhere. Then again, what would we expect from the One who is "...the life" (John 14:6).

The LORD gives her a caregiver! All of Naomi's fears about old age are laid to rest the moment Ruth "bare a son." For Naomi, Obed is going to be "a nourisher of thine old age." A "nourisher" puts bread and water on the table. When the years advance, Naomi will never have to worry about sustenance. Obed will take care of grandma!

Naomi's biting words tell us how "empty" the LORD has made her. But now, a little baby is a promise that her stomach will never be "empty." She looks into the face of a baby and knows, "God shall supply all your need" (Philippians 4:13).

The LORD gives her Ruth! When the presents are distributed on Christmas morning, most families save the best for last. So it is for Naomi. When she returns from Moab to Bethlehem, she indignantly moans, "I went out full, and the LORD hath brought me home again empty." It is a horrible statement. Standing next to her is one of the greatest women in world history. Standing next to her is a virtuous woman. Standing next to her is the Ruth of Ruth 1:16-17. How dare Naomi say, "I came home empty!"

The women of Bethlehem remind Naomi that Ruth is *"thy daughter in law."* For most of the *Book of Ruth*, we are told that Ruth is a pariah. She is a Moabitess and not like the rest of the people of Bethlehem. Nobody would want her in their family!

But all of that has changed. We can almost hear the ladies say, "That Naomi is so blessed to have Ruth for a daughter-in-law. I only wish that I were so fortunate!"

Chapter Twelve - Grandma!

The ladies inform Naomi that Ruth loves her. This is rather unusual. The Old Testament "rarely mentions a woman's love."[80] Even more powerful is the fact that for much of the story it is quite hard to find any love from Naomi to Ruth. Ruth's love is a merciful love that loves even when it is not returned. Had Naomi asked, "Why should Ruth love me so?" it would be difficult to find some good reasons.

Then there is the fact that Ruth is "better to thee than seven sons." The ideal Israelite family consisted of seven sons. The acknowledgement that Ruth was more valuable than seven sons is what one writer calls "extraordinary compensation."[81]

Another makes this intriguing point:

"The ancients strongly preferred sons to daughters. Hence, to say that one woman was worth seven men was the ultimate tribute—particularly in a story so absorbed with having a son!"[82]

We recall Naomi's tirade in Ruth 1:11-13:

And Naomi said, Turn again, my daughters: why will ye go with me? are there yet any more sons in my womb, that they may be your husbands? Turn again, my daughters, go your way; for I am too old to have an husband. If I should say, I have hope, if I should have an husband also to night, and should also bear sons; Would ye tarry for them till they were grown? would ye stay for them from having husbands? nay, my daughters; for it grieveth me much for your sakes that the hand of the LORD is gone out against me."

Naomi believes her life is ruined by the fact that her two sons are gone, and she is unable to bear another. Never did the thought cross her mind that one daughter-in-law from Moab could be better than two sons, let alone seven sons.

Yet before the curtain falls, there are two more amazing things to discover. In verse 16, the Bible says, "And Naomi took the child, and laid it in her bosom, and became nurse unto it." What a moment of bonding that must have been! We can well imagine the tears of joy flowing the first time Naomi holds little Obed so close to her heart. A lot of pain vanishes with such a tender moment.

Next, the neighbor ladies cannot contain their joy. "And the women her neighbours gave it a name, saying, There is a son born to Naomi; and they called his name Obed." It is the only naming ceremony in the Bible where females (other than the mother) are present.[83] It is the Old Testament version of a birth announcement, yet it comes with a strange twist. We would expect the ladies to say, "There is a son born to Ruth." Instead, they are proclaiming, "There is a son born to Naomi." The Bible is written as if Naomi is the mother and not the grandmother!

Chapter Twelve - Grandma!

It is quite the response. Naomi drags the Holy God of the Bible into the court of public opinion with her charges:

God is a bully.
God is unfair.
God is cruel.
God is unjust.
God is afflicting her.

When God finally answers these accusations, Ruth is holding a little Obed in her arms.

From Naomi to Mara to Grandma! What a story!

Chapter Thirteen

Marvelous Grace

When discussing the theme of the *Book of Ruth*, the default response always deals with redemption. It is the story of Boaz 'the redeemer' and Ruth 'the redeemed.' As we read these pages, something inside automatically begins to sing, "Redeemed, how I love to proclaim it!" It is a fascinating drama.

But when we look at the bigger story of Naomi vs. God, there is another song that leaps from these pages. We watch Naomi, who is so human, (and so much like us), hurl vitriol towards Heaven, and then we watch God respond in tender mercy and love. It brings us to the story of Calvary.

We, of course, are the little sheep who "have gone astray; we have turned every one to his own way" (Isaiah 53:6). Watching God give to Naomi, we can't help but remember "when we were yet without strength, in due time Christ died for the ungodly. For scarcely for a righteous man will one die: yet peradventure for a good man some would even dare to die. But God commendeth his love toward us, in that, while we were yet sinners, Christ died for us" (Romans 5:6-8). We watch the Savior gently and patiently woo Naomi, and we can hear "the Spirit and the bride say, Come. And let him that heareth say, Come. And let him that is athirst come. And whosoever will, let him take the water of life freely" (Revelation 22:17).

So the next time we read the *Book of Ruth*, perhaps we ought to break out and sing this old favorite:

Marvelous grace of our loving Lord,
Grace that exceeds our sin and our guilt!
Yonder on Calvary's mount outpoured
There where the blood of the Lamb was spilt.

Grace, grace, God's grace,
Grace that will pardon and cleanse within;
Grace, grace, God's grace,
Grace that is greater than all our sin![84]

In 1875, the beloved song writer, Fanny Crosby, had a desperate need of five dollars. As her custom, she bowed her head and gave her problem to the Lord. A few moments later, a stranger came to her door with the exact amount and handed it to her. Here is how she put it: "I have no way of accounting for this," she said, "except to believe that God put it into the heart of this good man to bring the money. My first thought was that it is so wonderful the way the Lord leads me, I immediately wrote a poem."[85]

We still sing those words:

All the way my Savior leads me;
What have I to ask beside?
Can I doubt His tender mercy,
Who through life has been my Guide?
Heavenly peace, divinest comfort,
Here by faith in Him to dwell!
For I know whate'er befall me,
Jesus doeth all things well.

All the way my Savior leads me,
Cheers each winding path I tread
Gives me grace for ev'ry trial,
Feeds me with the living bread.
Though my weary steps may falter,
And my soul athirst may be,
Gushing from the Rock before me,
Lo! a spring of joy I see.

All the way my Savior leads me;
Oh, the fullness of His love!
Perfect rest to me is promised
In my Father's house above.
When my spirit, clothed immortal,
Wings its flight to realms of day,
This my song through endless ages:
Jesus led me all the way.[86]

Ruth stands at the crossroads and makes a choice for the ages. She turns her back on her pagan idols, her lost family, her only hope of comfort and ease, and then she chooses to invest her life in the Will of God. Through all the loneliness, she never wavers and never turns back. Ruth can certainly join Fanny Crosby and sing, *"This my song through endless ages: Jesus led me all the way!"*

Naomi abandons her Bible in hopes that the world has a better offer. She learns the hard way that "thine own wickedness shall correct thee, and thy backslidings shall reprove thee: know therefore and see that *it is* an evil *thing* and bitter, that thou hast forsaken the LORD thy God, and that my fear *is* not in thee" (Jeremiah 2:19). Although she pays a hefty price for her choices, she can never exhaust the lovingkindness of her Savior. He gives and gives and gives again. When the dust settles, the Grace of God captures her heart.

So as the curtain falls on the Book of Ruth, we can hear Naomi singing as well: *"This my song through endless ages: Jesus led me all the way!"*

Chapter Fourteen
M&M's or Skittles

M&M's or Skittles?

Standing at the crossroads of life, Elimelech chooses to follow his wallet and not his Bible. Orpah teaches us that no choice is the wrong choice. Mr. Ho Suchaone reminds us that the selfish choice is the wrong choice. As for Boaz, he is yet another classic Bible illustration of the man willing to say, "I will serve the Lord." Saying 'yes' to the Bible is always the right choice. Then there is Naomi. She makes her choices and blames God for them.

We stand in admiration of the 'Moabitess' woman willing to put all on the 'altar of sacrifice.' Ruth stands at the candy counter and knows exactly what she wants. Her story is for the ages.

M&M's or Skittles

Long ago, as the story is told, there lived a king famous for his generosity. In the same city lived a simple beggar named Peter, whose great dream was to meet the king. He knew that if he would but ask, his king would bless him with a gift. One day it was announced that the king would visit his city, and Peter felt his dream would surely come true.

The great day came, and Peter made sure to be at the front of the excited crowd lining the street. Soon, the people heard singing and cheering as around the corner came the procession. There were soldiers, courtiers, drummers, and dancers, and, in the center, the king riding a fine horse.

As the procession drew near, Peter ran from the crowd to the middle of the street. Immediately, soldiers rushed to remove him, but the king called them back. He stopped his horse, handed the reins to an attendant, and walked towards Peter. A hush fell on the crowd, which soon changed to a gasp of surprise when the king went down on one knee before Peter. He put out his hand and said, "What gift will you give your king today?"

Peter was confused by the king's unexpected action. He was also disappointed and angry, but all eyes were on him. He pulled his begging sack from his shoulder, reached in among the bits and pieces, and felt some grains of corn. He took out one grain and slapped it in the king's hand.

Chapter Fourteen - M&M's or Skittles

The king showed no displeasure at the small gift. He accepted it graciously, walked back to his horse, and the procession resumed. Peter, disappointed and sulking, left the celebrations. He made his way home to his small hut, and angrily threw his begging sack on the floor. When it hit the floor, the contents spilled out.

Peter noticed something shining on the floor. He walked over, and there among the grains of corn, was a huge gold nugget. He stared in disbelief and wonder. The silence in the hut was broken by the noise of the celebration in the street, and he remembered his king. While he was giving his king a single grain of corn, the king had an attendant return a nugget of gold. He stood there in deep thought and finally said to himself, "Surely, he is so generous! I only wish I had given him more."

By and By when I look on His face,
Beautiful Face, thorn-shadowed Face;
By and By when I look on His face,
I'll wish I had given Him more.

More, so much more,
More of my life than I e'er gave before,
By and By when I look on his face,
I'll wish I had given Him more.

By and By when He holds out His hands,
Welcoming hands, nail-riven hands,

By and by when He holds out His hands,
I'll wish I had given Him more.

More, so much more,
More of my love than I e'er gave before,
By and by when he holds out his hands,
I'll wish I had given him more.

In the light of that heavenly place,
Light from his face, beautiful face,
In the light of that heavenly place,
I'll wish I had given him more.

More, so much more,
Treasures unbounded for Him I adore,
By and by when I look on his face,
I'll wish I had given him more.[87]

It is time for us to make our choices. We can live for Him, or we can live for self. We stand at the crossroads, but the clock is ticking. A decision has to be made. What will I do with my life?

M&M's or Skittles.

Endnotes

1. Hubbard, Robert. *The Book of Ruth - New International Commentary on the Old Testament*. Olivetree Edition. Eerdmans Publishing Company.
2. Reese, Edward. *KJV Reese Chronological Study Bible*. Baker Publishing Group. Kindle Edition.
3. To the Hebrew living in Old Testament times, only one land could be 'the land.' This is the land given to Abraham and his descendants.
4. Cundall, A. E., & Morris, L. (1968). *Judges and Ruth: an introduction and commentary* (Vol. 7, p. 239). Downers Grove, IL: InterVarsity Press.
5. Genesis 19:30-38; Numbers 22-24; Numbers 25:1-9; Deuteronomy 23:3-6; Judges 3:15-30.
6. Hubbard, Robert. *The Book of Ruth - New International Commentary on the Old Testament*. Olivetree Edition. Eerdmans Publishing Company.
7. "An Ammonite or Moabite shall not enter into the congregation of the LORD; even to their tenth generation shall they not enter into the congregation of the LORD for ever" (Deuteronomy 23:3).
8. Eskenazi, T. C., & Frymer-Kensky, T. (2011). *The JPS Bible Commentary: Ruth* (First edition, p. 4). Philadelphia, PA: Jewish Publication Society.
9. Rogers, A. (2017). It Is Decision that Determines Destiny. In *Adrian Rogers Sermon Archive* (Ru 1:1–18). Signal Hill, CA: Rogers Family Trust.
10. The popular TV star actually was named Orpah but people could not pronounce it correctly.
11. Smith, S., & Cornwall, J. (1998). In *The exhaustive dictionary of Bible names* (p. 189). North Brunswick, NJ: Bridge-Logos.
12. Eskenazi, T. C., & Frymer-Kensky, T. (2011). *The JPS Bible Commentary: Ruth* (First edition, p. 7). Philadelphia, PA: Jewish Publication Society.
13. Once again, the reference to "mother's house" and not father's house is interesting. While the family status of Orpah is unknown, Ruth's father was still alive (2:11). It is possible that the reference to "mother's house" implies the wish that they will soon remarry and go to their husband's house. If nothing else, it reinforces the caricature of Naomi.
14. Though we never read her name again, some Jewish rabbis in Old Testament times claim that Orpah had a great-grandson named Goliath! It may be the stuff that legends are made of, but the thought of the great-grandson of Ruth meeting the great-grandson of Orpah in the Valley of Elah is compelling! (Eskenazi, T. C., & Frymer-Kensky, T. (2011). *The JPS Bible Commentary: Ruth* (First edition, p. 17). Philadelphia, PA: Jewish Publication Society.)
15. https://talbottcampus.com/alcoholism-statistics/
16. Galaxie Software. (2002). *10,000 Sermon Illustrations*. Biblical Studies Press.
17. Five times in the book Ruth is referred to as a Moabitess.

18. Block, D. I. (1999). *Judges, Ruth* (Vol. 6, p. 634). Nashville: Broadman & Holman Publishers.
19. In addition to these ten occurrences, the same word in the Hebrew language reads as "gone back" in verse 15 and "brought me home" in verse 21.
20. Eskenazi, T. C., & Frymer-Kensky, T. (2011). *The JPS Bible Commentary: Ruth* (First edition, p. 26). Philadelphia, PA: Jewish Publication Society.
21. Cushing, William Orcutt (1896). From the hymn: *Under His Wings.*
22. Smith, Alfred B. (1981). Al Smith's Treasury of Hymn Histories. Greenville, SC: Better Music Publications.
23. Vine, W. E., Unger, M. F., & White, W., Jr. (1996). *Vine's Complete Expository Dictionary of Old and New Testament Words* (Vol. 1, p. 37). Nashville, TN: T. Nelson.
24. Block, Daniel I. (2015). *Ruth: A Discourse Analysis of the Hebrew Bible (The Zondervan Exegetical Commentary Series)*. Olivetree Edition. Grand Rapids: Zondervan Publishing.
25. Eskenazi, T. C., & Frymer-Kensky, T. (2011). *The JPS Bible Commentary: Ruth* (First edition, p. 21). Philadelphia, PA: Jewish Publication Society.
26. Ibid.
27. Cundall, A. E., & Morris, L. (1968). *Judges and Ruth: an introduction and commentary* (Vol. 7, p. 251). Downers Grove, IL: InterVarsity Press.
28. Eskenazi, T. C., & Frymer-Kensky, T. (2011). *The JPS Bible Commentary: Ruth* (First edition, p. 21). Philadelphia, PA: Jewish Publication Society.
29. 1 Samuel 3:17; 1 Samuel 14:44; 1 Samuel 20:13; 1 Samuel 25:22; 2 Samuel 3:9; 2 Samuel 3:35; 2 Samuel 19:13; 1 Kings 2:23; 1 Kings 19:2; 1 Kings 20:10; 2 Kings 6:31
30. Block, Daniel I. (2015). *Ruth: A Discourse Analysis of the Hebrew Bible (The Zondervan Exegetical Commentary Series)*. Olivetree Edition. Grand Rapids: Zondervan Publishing.
31. Green, M. P. (Ed.). (1989). *Illustrations for Biblical Preaching: Over 1500 sermon illustrations arranged by topic and indexed exhaustively* (Revised edition of: The expositor's illustration file). Grand Rapids: Baker Book House.
32. *The Ten Most Read Books in the World* by Jennifer Polland. Business Insider.
33. Rogers, A. (2017). The Romance of Redemption. In *Adrian Rogers Sermon Archive* (Ru 1–4). Signal Hill, CA: Rogers Family Trust.
34. Baker, W., & Carpenter, E. E. (2003). *The complete word study dictionary: Old Testament* (p. 662). Chattanooga, TN: AMG Publishers.
35. Reese, Edward. KJV Reese Chronological Study Bible (Kindle Locations 16416-16418). Baker Publishing Group. Kindle Edition.

Endnotes

36. Eskenazi, T. C., & Frymer-Kensky, T. (2011). *The JPS Bible Commentary: Ruth* (First edition, p. 95). Philadelphia, PA: Jewish Publication Society.
37. https://torah.org/learning/ruth-class41/
38. https://jwa.org/encyclopedia/article/Ruth-midrash-and-aggadah
39. The first words spoken by any Bible character should be noticed. They often are a commentary on his life.
40. Cundall, A. E., & Morris, L. (1968). *Judges and Ruth: an introduction and commentary* (Vol. 7, p. 263). Downers Grove, IL: InterVarsity Press.
41. This is quite the request. Normally, a widow would be allowed to glean the grain inadvertently left behind by the reapers. Ruth is asking to take her place among the harvesters. (Block)
42. The language of the Old Testament is quite emphatic. It is as if Boaz was pointing a finger at the ground and telling her, "Don't even think about leaving this field." (Hubbard)
43. Block, D. I. (1999). *Judges, Ruth* (Vol. 6, p. 670). Nashville: Broadman & Holman Publishers.
44. Eskenazi, T. C., & Frymer-Kensky, T. (2011). *The JPS Bible Commentary: Ruth* (First edition, p. 42). Philadelphia, PA: Jewish Publication Society.
45. Hubbard, Robert. *The Book of Ruth - New International Commentary on the Old Testament*. Olivetree Edition. Eerdmans Publishing Company.
46. https://deadline.com/2018/09/weather-channel-mike-seidel-hurricane-florence-exaggerates-1202465386/
47. https://www.psychologytoday.com/us/blog/communication-success/201406/how-spot-and-stop-manipulators
48. Block, D. I. (1999). *Judges, Ruth* (Vol. 6, p. 682). Nashville: Broadman & Holman Publishers.
49. Ibid.
50. Ezekiel 16:8-12
51. Given the setting at the threshing floor during the harvest, "eating and drinking" implies festivities, with "drinking" as reference to some intoxicating beverage (Eskenazi).
52. Block, D. I. (1999). *Judges, Ruth* (Vol. 6, pp. 685–687). Nashville: Broadman & Holman Publishers.
53. Three times in verse 4; Twice in verse 7, Verse 8,13,14.
54. Leviticus 18:6-19; Leviticus 20:11,17,19-21; Ezekiel 22:10; Deuteronomy 23:1; Deuteronomy 27:20. In the ancient world, to speak of a woman uncovering any part of a man's body at night (when that man is not her husband) was highly suggestive (Eskenazi)
55. Exodus 4:25; Judges 3:24; 1 Samuel 24:3; Deuteronomy 28:57; Ezekiel 16:25.
56. Block, D. I. (1999). *Judges, Ruth* (Vol. 6, pp. 685–687). Nashville: Broadman & Holman Publishers.

57. Baker, W., & Carpenter, E. E. (2003). *The complete word study dictionary: Old Testament* (p. 942). Chattanooga, TN: AMG Publishers.
58. Block, D. I. (1999). *Judges, Ruth* (Vol. 6, pp. 694–695). Nashville: Broadman & Holman Publishers.
59. Hubbard, Robert. *The Book of Ruth - New International Commentary on the Old Testament*. Olivetree Edition. Eerdmans Publishing Company.
60. Weber, C. P. (1999). 624 חול. R. L. Harris, G. L. Archer Jr., & B. K. Waltke (Eds.), *Theological Wordbook of the Old Testament* (electronic ed., p. 272). Chicago: Moody Press.
61. The question, "Who art thou," uses a feminine pronoun. Boaz knows a woman is there.
62. Crystal, David. Begat (Kindle Locations 3455-3456). OUP Oxford. Kindle Edition.
63. There is debate over the actual weight of the measure. Some claim that a measure was as much as 50 pounds, but it is unlikely that Ruth could carry away 300 pounds of grain in her vail. D.I. Block thinks it means six 'scoops' of barley.
64. Cundall, A. E., & Morris, L. (1968). *Judges and Ruth: an introduction and commentary* (Vol. 7, pp. 287–288). Downers Grove, IL: InterVarsity Press.
65. Baker, W., & Carpenter, E. E. (2003). *The complete word study dictionary: Old Testament* (p. 269). Chattanooga, TN: AMG Publishers.
66. Waard, J. de, & Nida, E. A. (1991). *A translator's handbook on the book of Ruth* (2nd ed., pp. 62–63). New York: United Bible Societies.
67. 1 Samuel 21:2; 2 Kings 6:8.
68. Block, D. I. (1999). *Judges, Ruth* (Vol. 6, p. 707). Nashville: Broadman & Holman Publishers.
69. Ibid.
70. Deuteronomy 25:5-10.
71. Block, D. I. (1999). *Judges, Ruth* (Vol. 6, p. 716). Nashville: Broadman & Holman Publishers.
72. Richardson, Bobby. Impact Player: Leaving a Lasting Legacy On and Off the Field (pp. 277-278). Tyndale House Publishers. Kindle Edition.
73. Whittier, John Greenleaf (1856). *Maud Muller*.
74. Smith, S., & Cornwall, J. (1998). In *The exhaustive dictionary of Bible names* (p. 187). North Brunswick, NJ: Bridge-Logos.
75. Phillips, John. Exploring the People of the Old Testament (Volume 2). Zondervan.
76. Block, D. I. (1999). *Judges, Ruth* (Vol. 6, p. 588). Nashville: Broadman & Holman Publishers.
77. Eskenazi, T. C., & Frymer-Kensky, T. (2011). *The JPS Bible Commentary: Ruth* (First edition, p. 88). Philadelphia, PA: Jewish Publication Society.
78. Hubbard, Robert. *The Book of Ruth - New International Commentary on the Old Testament*. Olivetree Edition. Eerdmans Publishing Company.

79. An example is found in the naming of Moses in Exodus 2:10.
80. Eskenazi, T. C., & Frymer-Kensky, T. (2011). *The JPS Bible Commentary: Ruth* (First edition, pp. 90–91). Philadelphia, PA: Jewish Publication Society.
The other women in the Old Testament are: Rebekah (Genesis 25:28); Michal (1 Samuel 18:20; 18:28: The Woman in the Song of Songs (Songs 1:7; 3:1-4)
81. Block, D. I. (1999). *Judges, Ruth* (Vol. 6, p. 729). Nashville: Broadman & Holman Publishers.
82. Hubbard, Robert. *The Book of Ruth - New International Commentary on the Old Testament*. Olivetree Edition. Eerdmans Publishing Company.
83. Block, D. I. (1999). *Judges, Ruth* (Vol. 6, p. 730). Nashville: Broadman & Holman Publishers.
84. Johnston, Julia H. (1911). *Grace Greater Than Our Sin.*
85. Osbeck, K. W. (1996). *Amazing grace: 366 inspiring hymn stories for daily devotions* (p. 259). Grand Rapids, MI: Kregel Publications.
86. Crosby, Fanny (1875). *All the Way My Savior Leads Me.*
87. Adkins, Grace Reese (1948). *I"ll Wish I Had Given Him More.*

Books By Paul Schwanke

Major Messages from Minor Prophets Series

Magnify the Word Series

Evangelist Paul Schwanke
www.preachthebible.com

Made in the USA
Columbia, SC
01 October 2021